Straight
Talking

Straight
Talking

Learn how to
overcome insomnia, anxiety,
negative thinking and other
modern-day stresses

Linda Blair

PIATKUS

First published in Great Britain in 2008 by Piatkus Books
This paperback edition published in 2009 by Piatkus
Reprinted 2011

A CIP catalogue record for this book
is available from the British Library.

ISBN 978-0-7499-2955-8

Typeset in ITC Stone Serif by Palimpsest Book Production Limited,
Grangemouth, Stirlingshire
Printed in the UK by CPI Mackays, Chatham ME5 8TD

Piatkus
An imprint of
Little, Brown Book Group
100 Victoria Embankment
London EC4Y 0DY

An Hachette UK Company
www.hachette.co.uk

www.piatkus.co.uk

To Rob, Jonathan, Sam and Katy.
Those you love teach you the most.

Acknowledgements

I have so many people to thank that I'm wondering where to start. I'll begin, I think, with my teachers. Those who really made learning exciting, and who made me want to know everything I can are: Robert Hinde, Howard Gardener, Michael Rutter, Jerry Kagan, Roger Brown, John Teasdale and Mark Williams. You have a real gift for inspiring others. Thank you.

I owe so much, too, to my friends for their unwavering support and affection, and for reminding me during the tough times that life is actually pretty good. Thank you Frances Hedgeland, Fiona Goodwille, Ellen Winner, Daphne Astor, Janet Reibstein, Julie Kaufman, Corinne Goldstein, Dena Kleiman, Randy Roy, Nick Barraclough and Joanna Gates.

I want to give special thanks to my brother Paul, my sister Christen ('I do it MYSELF!') and my Aunt Augusta (yes, I really do have one). They've shown me the sort of blind faith that only family can offer.

Then, of course, I owe an enormous debt to my patients. Thank you, all of you, for sharing your lives so honestly with me.

My gratitude also goes to my professional team. You all encouraged me to put what I've learned into this book, and you helped me give it shape: Gill Bailey, Judy Piatkus, Jo Brooks and Jillian Stewart at Piatkus Books; my agents Molly Stirling and Nicola Ibison; and my friend, colleague and ace photographer Jeannette Josse.

I want to extend the warmest and most special thanks to Maureen Rice, my editor at *Psychologies*. Your absolute, un-wavering belief that I could write has given me the courage to do so. Thank you, Maureen.

Finally, my biggest thank you goes to my children Katy, Sam and Jonathan and to his wife Helen, and most of all to my husband Rob. I feel so lucky to be sharing my life with all of you.

Linda Blair

Born into a medical family in Missouri, Linda grew up in Kansas. At 18 she attended Wellesley College in Massachusetts, where she discovered her passion for psychology and literature. After graduating in psychology, she moved to England for three years. For part of this time she worked in the animal-behaviour unit at Cambridge University studying mother–infant relationships in primates with Professor Robert Hinde. This convinced her to study developmental psychology, and she was awarded a scholarship at Harvard to study children's play and linguistic development. She returned to London in 1978 to begin her clinical psychology training, qualifying as a clinical psychologist in 1980 after studying at the Maudsley Hospital. After studying German in Munich that summer, she returned to Cambridge to take up an NHS post working with the elderly.

Two years later she took up another NHS job, this time working with children and their families. She adopted her first son, Jonathan, during this period and switched from full-time to part-time work.

Over the next 15 years, as her family size increased from one to three children, Linda worked in a number of part-time jobs for the NHS, the Medical Research Council and University of Cambridge. She also started a private practice as a clinical psychologist specialising in cognitive therapy, and began lecturing to students in schools and universities on how to cope with exam stress, both of which she continues with today.

In 2000, with her children and her husband, she moved to Bath, where she worked in the University of Bath Medical Centre, offering cognitive therapy to students and staff. By the end of 2004 her writing and media work had become so time-consuming that she resigned her university position.

Her writing and media career began by chance, in Cambridge, in the 1980s. The local BBC radio station asked the local psychology department if someone was available to join a discussion about phobias. Linda was the only psychologist free, and so she joined in. She was asked to return for a regular weekly programme, and now broadcasts frequently on radio, including Radios 4 and 2, BBC Radio Wales and the World Service. She has also appeared in a number of television shows including: *Child of Our Time*, *Mindshock* (about children raised without human language), *Yesterday Once More* (the life of Karen Carpenter), *Kilroy*, and *The Ruby Wax Show*. She's quoted regularly in newspapers and magazines, and has a weekly column in the *Guardian*, and monthly columns in *Psychologies* and *Junior* magazines.

Linda is a member of the media committee, which the British Psychological Society recommends to the press, television and radio commentators. Her professional qualifications include chartered status with the British Psychological Society (she is an Associate Fellow). She's also a Chartered Scientist. Her chief interests are her family, her dogs, sport (particularly swimming and walking), cooking, gardening, literature and just about anything psychological.

Contents

Foreword

As editor of *Psychologies* magazine, I've spent the past few years reading and assessing 'self-help' and popular psychology books of all kinds. In that time I've discovered that a good book really can help transform your life – but also that there are far more bad books of this kind than good ones. This is a shame, because life is too short to waste on books written by egotistical 'gurus' who promise instant results and peddle over-hyped, invented 'formulas' for success. A good self-help book involves none of those things, and *Straight Talking* is one of the very best. It is 'self help' at its purest and most honest – it provides knowledge and insights that allow us to, literally, help ourselves to a genuinely happier, more fulfilled life.

Straight Talking is, above all, a practical book that can deliver exactly what it promises: relief from insomnia, anxiety, negative thinking and other modern stresses – the kind of problems that bother pretty much all of us at some point. It's based on a rigorously tested set of tools and treatments that Linda Blair has used for many years as a clinical psychologist, successfully treating people just like you and me. She knows what she's doing and has years of practice and solid science to back her up. This then is a book you can trust.

It's also a straightforward book and if I didn't already love it for being so practical, I would love it for this alone. You'll look in vain for any hint of 'guru talk' here. Linda knows a great deal about the thoughts and behaviours that make us unhappy and unproductive, and the best ways to overcome those problems, but she never pretends, even for a moment, that this makes her some kind of magician. Instead, she shares the best and most reliable tools and techniques as just that: tools for us to use as we think best.

If Linda stands for anything, it is her absolute commitment to the idea of personal responsibility and self-reliance. We and we alone are the makers and masters of our lives. She respects knowledge, but is dismissive of 'expert worship' because although we can all use the knowledge the experts have, when it comes to the subject of you, then you know more. There is real and important information that can help anyone, but it belongs to all of us – it should not be the preserve of the experts. In *Straight Talking* she shares that knowledge and helps us to adapt it to our own lives and experiences, so that we can make a real difference to our quality of life.

I first met Linda several years ago, when I was writing about personal development and emotional health, and used to call her for some expert support and background. Like most properly qualified psychologists and therapists she knew her subject well – but unlike many other experts, she knew how to talk about it so that other people could easily understand it too. Speaking to Linda was like having an ordinary – if absolutely riveting and inspiring – conversation. She never uses jargon, she often uses humour, but above all, she has a uniquely 'Linda' way of getting straight to the heart of the matter – to uncover the essence of a point or a concept and describe it in a way that is instantly understandable and illuminating. Linda has knowledge, experience, compassion and what used to be called plain good sense. She knows as much as anyone I've ever met about the art and science of living well. But her greatest gift is her ability to communicate – generously, honestly and openly – and give us all the tools to help ourselves to fuller, happier lives.

Maureen Rice
Editor, *Psychologies* Magazine
March 2008

Introduction

You're probably wondering why I've written a book that tells
you how to solve psychological problems, when at the same
time I'm encouraging you to trust yourself when it comes to
solving such problems.

The reason is that this book isn't the usual sort of self-help
book. In this book, you won't find a 'one-size-fits-all' regime.
There's no diet plan, no fitness routine, no one method that
promises inner peace. Instead, you're going to find lots of
suggestions and ideas, laid out in the way my patients have
told me is most useful, so you can choose for yourself what
will help you most.

You see, I believe you'll have the best chance of living as
you'd like to live if we work together as equals. I know a
great deal about the psychological difficulties that get in the
way of self-confidence and a sense of personal fulfilment.
You, on the other hand, know more than anyone else in the
world about the person we're concerned about. Together we'll
make a good team. Together we can discover the best ways

for you to deal effectively with problems that may have troubled you for years, problems such as an inability to sleep restfully, a tendency to let anxiety get in the way of clear thinking, or a habit of fearing the worst and avoiding challenges rather than expecting the best and daring to try something new.

The suggestions I'll be offering you are the fruits of 25 years of clinical work. I've worked in research establishments in America and in England, in the NHS, in schools and universities, in Social Services and in private practice. The people who've come to see me are from all sorts of backgrounds, and they've had all sorts of different experiences. They've been referred by their doctors, their specialists, their teachers or employers, or their friends. Their problems range from unexplained fatigue, to cripplingly low self-esteem, to an inability even to step outside the house without experiencing the most severe panic attack. Some of them have struggled with their problems for several weeks, others for many years.

With time, I began to realise that I was hearing the same themes in my clinics: that whatever their diagnoses, people were wanting help with the same problems. Almost everyone, for example, complained of difficulty in sleeping and of an inability to control feelings of anxiety. Most wanted to find ways to think positively rather than negatively, and to feel contented rather than dissatisfied. Many spoke of a desire to leave their past behind them so that they could feel free to move forward. Often they would tell me that they had coped well for a time but then relapsed, and, as a result, experienced an even greater drop in self-confidence.

I also began to realise that the people who came to see me had stopped believing that they had any power at all to help themselves. They'd given up expecting to overcome their own difficulties, and they were hoping that someone else would simply step in and sort them out. Gemma is a good example of what I mean: she was so eager to start our first session that she was already talking before we'd even sat down.

'I'm so glad you were able to see me. My GP said there'd be a wait, but here I am. I know you'll sort me out now.'

I thought we really ought to slow things down a bit. 'What were you hoping we might work on together?' I began.

'Together? Yes, of course. I'll do whatever you tell me to do. I just need you to sort me out – you know, everything, really.'

This wasn't, alas, an unusual first exchange. It seems that we've become convinced that the 'experts' are the only ones who have the answers to our problems. We expect them to give us a diagnosis and a formula so that we can take it home with us, much like a prescription, and then all will be well.

But I'm afraid that all won't be well, at least not for long, unless you become involved both in creating and in testing out your own cure. It's much easier, I know, to put yourself in the hands of some 'expert', as Gemma wanted to do, and simply wait passively to receive a ready-made solution. All too often, we therapists don't discourage that kind of attitude because it feels so good to be admired and needed. But if you want to achieve really lasting improvements, you'll have to take a leading role in making them happen.

That's how this book will help you. I've identified six problem areas and each is defined at the beginning of Chapter 2 through to Chapter 7. I'll explain why that problem may have become part of your life, and what may be keeping it going even when it seems only to make things worse for you. Then I'll offer a number of suggestions that can help you deal effectively with it. Finally, I'll also describe how some of my patients (real names and personal details changed to protect their privacy) have solved their problems – how they've adapted general suggestions to fit exactly into their own lives – to give you some ideas that will help you start sorting out your own dilemmas.

Then your own work begins. The treatment manual that you create will be like no other. You'll choose the suggestions that appeal to you, test them out and modify them until they fit your own circumstances precisely.

Throughout the book, I've tried hard to avoid jargon and to describe things as simply and directly as possible. I don't believe there's any need to make things complicated, because fancy words don't solve problems. That's why, in fact, I've called the book *Straight Talking*. My aim has been to create a method that will make sense to you whether you've had therapy or not, or whether you're acquainted with psychological jargon or not. And, after all, this book should earn its title, don't you think?

This approach will be relevant for you, whether or not you have a diagnosable psychological problem. Most of us have to deal with high levels of stress these days, whether it's through demands at work or in our various relationships and complicated family arrangements, and as a result most of us know all too well about sleeplessness, anxiety and negative thinking. Because these problems are, unfortunately, now almost universal, there ought to be something useful in here for almost everyone.

However, before we start tackling the problems that are common to so many of us, I want to give you a little background. Therefore, Chapter 1 talks about why so many of us seem to have lost confidence in our own coping mechanisms and in our own sense of self-direction. How did we become so dependent on others to tell us what to do? When did we stop feeling responsible for the course our lives can take? Why do we so often look anywhere but within ourselves when we try to sort out our problems?

The rest of the book is devoted to the problems themselves. I present them in the same order that I would work on them with you if you had come to see me for therapy. Of course, you needn't follow this order exactly, and not all of the problems will apply to you. But if you're troubled by more than one of these issues – and many of us are – then I suggest that you deal with them in the order in which I've presented them.

The most immediate stumbling blocks to living a fulfilling life are an inability to sleep restfully and the mental chaos created by chronic anxiety. These two almost always occur together, so I expect that you'll want to read both Chapters 2 and 3. Because sleep disturbance and anxiety interfere with your powers of concentration, attention and memory, it's difficult to think sensibly about anything else, so it's advisable for you to deal with these problems first.

Of course, not many psychologists could avoid talking about the role that your past plays in determining your psychological health. If that past contains negative or hurtful moments, how can you free yourself from them? This is what I'll talk about in Chapter 4, although not perhaps in the ways that you might expect.

Next, in Chapter 5, we'll look at what stops you from thinking beyond your day-to-day problems, preventing you from making positive plans and from chasing your dreams. Do you focus only on what could go wrong, discounting or minimising the good things that also happen? Do you underestimate your strong points and concentrate primarily on what you can't do? Does it seem to you that the world is full of disasters just waiting to happen, or that everyone else copes brilliantly except you? If so, this chapter, which talks about the negative mindset and what you can do to change it, is for you.

But even if your thinking is fairly logical and your attitude is reasonably positive, do you still feel restless or unfulfilled? How might you go about finding contentment in your life? How can you carve out moments of peace? How can you know what 'enough' is? These are the issues we'll examine in Chapter 6.

Finally, there's the question of what to do if you slip backwards. Your first reaction would probably be to assume that you've somehow failed. But relapse, the subject of Chapter 7, is a normal and totally acceptable part of living. You'll never really go back to square one – you simply stumble sometimes.

I want to show you that a relapse is merely an amber light, a wake-up call telling you that it's time to stop, rethink and become a bit more refined in your knowledge of yourself.

If you've worked on any of the preceding problems as I've suggested, you'll find you've already done most of the preparatory work necessary to recover from a relapse. As a result, you'll find that the work you have to do in this chapter is less than it was in any of the others.

Chapter 8 contains the Resources and Suggested Reading. I've set them out in an unconventional way, but in a way that I hope you'll find will enrich your understanding of whatever problems you want to tackle. As any of my patients will tell you, additional reading is an important part of the recommendations I make in therapy. This is all part of my desire to empower you. After all, if you read what I've read, then you can interpret the information directly, rather than having to rely on what I think the work is trying to say. So what I've done is to collect the sources that will interest you most, and after each one I'll describe briefly which problems that particular reference targets best.

I want you to use this book in much the same way that you would use a good cookbook. Read the chapters that interest you, the ones that seem most relevant to your life. Then choose the suggestions in those chapters that appeal, and make them your own. Keep notes of your starting point and the improvements you make, as well as how you've modified any suggestions you use and how they've helped you.

In effect, I'll be helping you to write your own treatment manual. Your solutions, and the resulting pride and increased self-confidence you'll feel, will be well worth the effort.

Remember, things can always improve.

1

How Did We Get Here?

My youngest sister was the most fiercely independent child that I'd ever known. Her first sentence, 'I do it MYSELF!' says it all.

Today she lives in Montana in a house that she and her husband built with their own hands. She grows most of the food they need, canning, drying and freezing it so that it lasts through the winter. They keep chickens to supply their eggs and meat. They live in a stable community where everyone swaps skills and equipment. They haven't much money, it's true, and they rarely travel. Yet she's one of the happiest and most self-confident people I know.

The link between figuring out how to solve your own problems on the one hand, and contentment and self-confidence on the other, is a strong one. And what's even more intriguing is that the converse appears also to be true. That is, the less you understand about how things in your daily life were created and how they work, and the more you rely on others to sort you out, the more vulnerable you are to low self-esteem rather than confidence, and to anxiety rather than contentment.

Of course, there's no need to go to my sister's extremes to prove your independence. But if there was a return to greater self-sufficiency generally it would, in my opinion, be a very good thing.

The trend away from self-reliance is quite recent. Only 50 or 60 years ago my sister's way of life wouldn't have been so unusual. Why, then, has there been such a rapid and enormous change?

There's no simple answer. Instead, I think there are a number of contributory reasons that, taken together, have stopped us expecting that we can solve our problems ourselves. None of these reasons is totally bad in itself, nor has any one of them brought us to our present state. These factors are all working together, and in terms of human happiness they're not helping us much at all.

So what, then, are these factors? I've included those that I feel are important:

1 Information overload

Once upon a time the only way to transmit information was for one person to show another one how to do something. Human beings are designed to learn best in this manner, and I believe it's still the most effective and the most natural method we have for communicating and mastering new information. If you doubt this, just spend some time observing small children. They watch, they copy and they learn – very, very quickly.

The biggest change in the way we share information took place when writing was invented. For the first time, knowledge could stand alone, without another person being present to transmit it. The invention of the printing press was the next big step. This allowed copies of information to be made quickly and easily. Today, electronic storage and transmission of material has once again changed our ability to access information. The amount that's available is now absolutely vast, it's growing literally by the second and it's available instantaneously.

Nowadays you can find information on just about anything

almost immediately, and, as a result, we've come to expect answers more or less straightaway. We tend to forget that not much of this information has been analysed properly. But instead of challenging, comparing and criticising what we're offered, we've only become more impatient. We no longer feel we should have to take the time to adapt, modify and challenge what we're told. We've forgotten that advice is always general and needs to be adapted if we want to use it, because we ourselves remain individuals.

One complication is that even if we decide to approach what we're offered with a critical eye, it's difficult to find anyone who can help us. There are a growing number of experts in just about anything, but it's difficult to find someone who claims to have general knowledge. The specialists are often so immersed in their area of expertise that they've lost the wider picture. They may not know how their own field relates to other areas of knowledge, or even how it can be applied to everyday, real-life situations.

The result is that the vast store of information, easily available but not really sorted, contextualised or evaluated, hasn't empowered us as we'd hoped. Instead, it often becomes just another source of anxiety and confusion.

2 The speed of scientific advancement

Recent achievements in all areas of science – medicine, biology, genetics and physics, to name but a few – are truly staggering. It's now possible to keep people alive while in a persistent vegetative state, to create life in laboratories and even to combine the genetic material of different species. However, the problem once again is that these breakthroughs are taking place far too quickly. No one seems able to afford the time to evaluate the achievements ethically, to legislate regarding their applications thoughtfully or, sometimes, even to test their safety adequately.

Innovations in science and technology can be applied equally to good or evil ends, so it's important that we take the time to consider, debate and evaluate each advance before deciding how best to apply and to limit it. But, because there seems to be some sort of headlong blind rush simply to keep advancing for the sake of it, this isn't happening. We can now know something is possible long before it's available. We often hear of new advances, but without reference to whether they'll help us or harm us. This disconnection between science and technology on the one hand, and morality and ethics on the other, is causing anxiety and discontent, particularly in the biological sciences where the very definitions of 'life' and 'death' are being disputed.

3 Ease of mobility

Humans are social animals. We need each other for practical help as well as for emotional security, and it takes time for us to build the bonds of trust. This wasn't such a concern in the days when travel was slow and difficult, because we remained with the same people for most of our lives. Now it's easy to travel vast distances, and, as a result, there have been all kinds of changes in the way businesses are run and in the expectations that we have about where we might live. This makes stable and enduring relationships more difficult to maintain, leaving us feeling unsupported and alone. These feelings of isolation are associated with anxiety, sleep disturbance and negative thinking.

Take for example the way we work. Until quite recently it was possible and, in fact, fairly common to spend an entire career working within one company, and, moreover, to have that entire career based in one location. This is rare now. Relocation is often required. Many jobs have short fixed-term contracts and redundancy is common. You may have to look for work in several different locations, and probably also to be employed by a number of different companies during the course of your working life. This makes it harder to build up a sense of community and feel rooted and secure.

Under such conditions it's also hard to forge long-term friendships with colleagues, or to follow the careers of those who could serve as role models at work. Uncertainty in the workplace also means that you're more likely to look upon those you work with as potential rivals rather than as colleagues who can support and help you. Increased specialisation and rapid changes in technology mean that we have continually to change the way we work. This, too, can contribute to feelings of inadequacy. It's not hard to see why employment has become a major source of stress for many of us.

And, of course, if work requires you to move about frequently, there are fewer opportunities to build a sense of community where you live. You probably don't see much point in getting to know the people next door if you know you're likely to move away soon. Family and childhood friends, too, are likely to be scattered far and wide. It's no wonder that there are so many dating services springing up, and that websites like Friends Reunited (see Chapter 8, Resources and Suggested Reading) are flourishing. It's natural to feel most secure, confident and contented when you're surrounded by a supportive social network. Without it, you become vulnerable to bouts of loneliness, insecurity and anxiety.

4 The trend towards living alone

It's been predicted that within the next 30 years, more than a third of the British population will be living alone. These individuals won't just be older people whose partners have died, as you might suppose. In fact, the fastest growing category is made up of people aged 35 to 44, particularly men.

It's not clear why this is so. Perhaps there's a growing fear of marriage and cohabitation because of the financial consequences such commitments carry if the relationship breaks down. Perhaps uncertainty in the job market encourages individuals in this age group to focus on their careers to the exclusion of other relationships.

One of the consequences of being alone is that you can easily lose your sense of proportion. Without someone to reassure you or to allow you to talk things through, small worries start to seem bigger and to appear more significant than they actually are. This sort of mindset breeds anxiety and negative thinking, and it can sometimes even result in panic attacks.

It's also easier, when you're alone, to fall into fixed patterns of behaviour. Bad habits may become well entrenched before you realise what a negative effect they're having on you. It can then feel overwhelmingly difficult to break those bad habits. This, of course, feeds negative thinking, and it can be much harder to recover from relapses.

5 Too many interruptions

There's been a recent surge of interest in meditation, mindfulness (paying attention carefully and in detail to your immediate surroundings or your breathing) and other techniques designed to quieten the mind – and I'm not surprised. We're living in an environment that's increasingly noisy and that invites continual interruptions to our thoughts. We carry mobile phones, personal stereos, iPods, Blackberries and so on, all capable of interrupting our thoughts unpredictably. A survey in 2007 of over 4,000 Americans revealed that over 60 per cent of them take their electronic gadgets to bed with them, and nearly 40 per cent said they'd replied to emails in the middle of the night. Eighty-three per cent said they check their emails while on holiday.

And even if you turn off all these personal communication gadgets, you're still faced with musak, intercom paging and advertising at every turn. Frequent and unpredictable interruptions are known to interfere with concentration. I'm sure they're a major contributor to the reported rise in levels of sleep disturbance and anxiety.

6 The power of the media

Newspapers, magazines, television, radio broadcasting and advertisements – the media is probably the most powerful unelected body in modern life. It may even be the most powerful body of them all. It's around us all the time and everywhere. Surveys have shown that product symbols and brands used in advertising – for example the McDonald's golden arches and the Coca-Cola logo – are now recognised more readily around the world than are any other symbols in existence. And we're likely to know, or at least think we know, more about the lives of celebrities than we do about the lives of our own next-door neighbours.

One of the biggest drawbacks about the information that's delivered to us through the media is that it's often presented out of context. For example, when two girls in East Anglia were kidnapped and murdered in 2001, parents all over Britain became highly anxious because they feared that this same fate might befall their own children. That wasn't surprising, as few, if any, of the stories covering this horrible event reminded readers and viewers of how mercifully rare such crimes are. Likewise, reports of aeroplane or train crashes frighten the public (temporarily) away from travelling by those methods because the rarity of such disasters is never mentioned. This focus on the few times when there are accidents draws our attention away from the fact that most aeroplane and train journeys are completed without incident.

The way the media focuses on bad news makes more sense

if we bear in mind that its aim is not to present a balanced picture. The aim of media is to sell itself. Therefore, the more common and less interesting events are rarely reported, whereas bizarre or frightening (and therefore fascinating) occurrences are described in detail. Unless we take the time to put the events we hear about into their proper context, we end up with an extremely skewed picture of the world – and it can look like a very dangerous place. And, of course, that's one of the media's intentions. If you think you might be in danger, you're likely to feel the need to learn more about what you're up against so that you can be better prepared to deal with it. You'll want to seek out more details and updates from the media so that you can keep yourself informed. This vicious circle fills the media coffers, but it doesn't really add much to your sense of personal security or self-reliance.

Another problem with media presentation is that the information offered is only a very small part of the whole story, and, in practical terms, you can understand why. There's never sufficient space or time, nor is it deemed practical, to present the entire picture. The result is that those of us on the receiving end see only a snapshot, yet we think we've seen the whole film.

But even that wouldn't be so worrying if what we were given was a fair representation. Unfortunately, that's almost never the case. This is nowhere more obvious than when the lives of the celebrities are discussed. Even their photographs are selective or enhanced – usually both. And when we see what appears to be so exciting and wonderful, we want to have the same things that they have and to live like they do. We start feeling envious and deprived with what may previously have seemed perfectly adequate to us. We're never told, however, how much luck was involved in getting those celebrities to where they are, nor do we see the effort that they really have to put in. We think it must be easy to have all this. Then when we don't achieve stardom or get rich or whatever, we become disillusioned and discontented, and feel that somehow we're failing.

7 Confusing wanting with needing

Most modern Western economies are based on acquisition. The argument is that as long as there's a demand, industry will keep producing goods, and, of course, making profits for the company owners and shareholders. Therefore, companies need to make sure we want more and more of whatever they are selling. One effective way to do this is to encourage us to think that we need things that aren't really needed – in other words, to confuse needing with wanting. Advertisers constantly tell us that it's a 'good idea' to have this or that, that we really ought to get hold of this week's 'must have' and that we should 'spend and save'. With all this continual pressure, it's easy to lose sight of the fact that the only things that we really need are adequate food, water, warmth and shelter, and that all the rest are actually luxuries that should be considered as such. However, because that way of thinking doesn't fuel an expanding economy or line the pockets of profiteers, we aren't given this message.

At last, and I hope in time, we've woken up to the fact that this attitude is literally destroying the earth. Let me add that it's also destroying our sense of contentment, and it's feeding our anxiety.

8 The fear of growing older

'Beauty is Truth, truth beauty' – *that is all*
Ye know on earth, and all ye need to know.
'Ode on a Grecian Urn'
John Keats

Substitute 'youth' for 'Truth' and you've captured a basic modern belief. Cosmetics, fashion, crash diets, cosmetic surgery: they all carry the message that it's vital to look as youthful as possible. Instead of viewing old age as a time of reflection and wisdom, the implication is that it's a time of loss and pain, a time to fear and to avoid.

Everywhere we turn, we're encouraged to hide any signs of ageing. If ever there was a way to engender a sense of helplessness, despair and discontent, this is surely the one. We might, at great effort and vast expense, delay some of the signs of ageing, but we can't avoid them altogether. There's no escaping time. Youth worship is only making us unhappy. If, instead, we'd value each stage of life for its own special characteristics, rather than pinning all our dreams on just the one brief chapter, how much happier we'd all feel!

Old age does bring loss and pain, it's true – but it also confers a greater ability to deal with these things. When we're older, we're free from the pressures of growing, mating and reproduction, so we have time to reflect on and organise what our experiences have taught us. At last, too, we have time to share the experiences we've gained and impart the lessons we've learned, and because each of us is different, we'll each have something unique to contribute.

9 The loss of real play time

The child psychologist Jean Piaget once said that 'In order for a child to understand something . . . he must construct it himself; he must reinvent it.' He was making the distinction here between learning and true understanding.

You can learn pretty much anything. By that I mean you can memorise and repeat what you see or hear if you practise it often enough, even when it doesn't mean anything to you. But in order to understand something fully, you'll need to take it apart, order it, reorder it and put it back together. And it's understanding, rather than learning, that's linked with a sense of competence and self-confidence.

The most enjoyable way to acquire understanding is through play. Playing is all about creating, imagining, assembling and rearranging, without a predetermined goal in mind. It's the best way we have, not only to understand, but also to create. The majority of our most useful and important breakthroughs have occurred when individuals 'played around' with ideas and looked at things in new ways. That's how, for example, Pasteur learned the value of heating milk, and Fleming discovered penicillin.

Sadly, however, much of what's out there to 'play' with today is already formed and assembled, and you're simply supposed to react to it. Watching endless reruns and remakes on television may rest the mind temporarily, and playing computer games may encourage quicker reaction times or better hand–eye co-ordination, but these activities won't encourage you to acquire deeper understanding or to create something new. If you want to feel competent or energised with new ideas it's far better to spend some time trying out a new recipe, mending a broken toy, or debating with friends than it is to sit in front of a television or computer screen. There's nothing inherently wrong with television or computer screens, it's just that we're spending far too much time in their company.

To understand the way the world works and to feel capable of solving problems, we need unstructured time. This is particularly true for children, for if they aren't allowed these opportunities, they'll never learn to direct themselves.

Summary

I hope this discussion has pointed out some of the social and technological reasons why you may be feeling anxious, discontented and beset with negative thoughts. Too much information, presented without much editing or organising, can easily overwhelm you. Divorcing science from ethics makes the world feel unsafe. Ease of mobility means that it's now more difficult to build and maintain the relationships that you need to feel stable and secure. The lack of realistic role models makes it hard for you to imagine satisfying ways of living, and the continual, insistent messages that you don't have enough can cause you to feel deprived and discontented. Constant interruptions will prevent you from solving problems or dreaming about new possibilities. An impossible race against time will merely exhaust your resources and energy pointlessly. And, no time for creative play means that innovative problem solving has become all too rare.

It's tiring to confront these factors continually, and it can make it more difficult – and sometimes seemingly impossible – to take on board any new challenges in your daily life. That's what happened to the individuals I describe in the case histories at the end of each chapter. The event that tips the balance is most likely to be something distressing, as it was for three of the individuals I describe – the death of a parent, a child leaving home, a relocation. But the trigger event can sometimes be a welcome occurrence, such as a job promotion. The point is that the trigger event calls for change and readjustment, and if you're already feeling isolated or overloaded, one more stress is simply one stress too many. This is why I believe that for treatment to be successful, the effects of the factors I've described need to be addressed as well as the trigger event.

However, you don't have to feel anxious or helpless in the face of this. Nor is there any need to go to extremes, such as returning to some sort of primitive state, to escape it all. The changes in our world may have happened too fast, but they're not necessarily bad in themselves. What's important is how you regard them and how you use them. The suggestions and techniques I offer throughout the book will help you to stay strong and centred, so these factors need not unbalance you.

Remember that the human psyche hasn't changed much, even though the world around us has. You still need to take the time to criticise and evaluate what you're told before you accept it. You still need to obtain at least part of your learning through direct observation and instruction. You still need to prioritise your relationships and to invest time in them, and work to build communities that are made up of people who care about and trust each other. You need to shut out unnecessary interruptions on a regular basis, and make time to play with no particular aim in mind, in order to see where it takes you. Such changes in your behaviour and your attitudes will go a long way towards restoring your self-confidence, your sense of optimism and feelings of contentment, and the ability to trust yourself when you face challenges.

But even armed with these changes, it won't necessarily be easy to start living your life as fully as you'd wish. Problems are inevitable, although a defeatist attitude towards them is not. All you need to do is to regard the problems you face as challenges that you can meet, and to start looking for ways to do so.

We're now going to examine some of today's most common psychological problems and consider ways that you can deal effectively with them. I'll suggest a number of techniques, and you'll then have the opportunity to fashion them into your own solutions.

This book is intended as a beginning, a means of kick starting you so that you can travel your own way. Very soon, I hope you'll be feeling that you're more in charge of your own life direction. At that point you'll be able to experience a most wonderful feeling, the unbeatable sense of self-reliance and self-confidence that comes when you can say, 'I do it MYSELF!'

2

Sleep Disturbance

Sleep that knits up the ravell'd sleeve of care,
The death of each day's life, sore labour's bath,
Balm of hurt minds, great nature's second course,
Chief nourisher in life's feast.

Macbeth, II. ii

Sleeplessness: there's no other torment that can rob us so reliably of reason and hope. No other problem prevents clear thinking and logical problem solving so effectively. The average person should expect to spend a quarter to a third of every 24 hours asleep, recovering mentally and physically and preparing to think clearly the next day. But, sadly, for many that much recovery time is a luxury – the exception rather than the rule. We face increasing demands at work and at home, and we feel as if we must do everything faster, even as we find ourselves in the midst of more noise and distractions. There seems to be less time available to wind down and relax, let alone to sleep.

In fact, sleep disturbance is such a widespread and distressing problem that it's considered to be a separate category of mental disorder itself. I won't, however, be talking specifically about any of the problems that fall within this category, problems such as narcolepsy, hypersomnia, and nightmare disorder. These are interesting, but they're relatively rare. Nonetheless, individuals suffering from such disorders may find some of the suggestions in this chapter helpful.

What I'll be focusing on instead is the much more common type of sleep disturbance, the sort of difficulty that you've almost certainly experienced at some point. This is the definition I have in mind when I talk about a sleep disorder: *regularly feeling unable to sleep for as long as you feel you need to sleep or would like to sleep, despite having the opportunity to do so.*

In particular, I'll be focusing on sleep problems that have become established, and by that I mean they've been troubling you for more than three weeks without relief. In these cases, the problem has now become a habit, and that means it will persist simply because it's become a familiar way of behaving, even though it's uncomfortable.

I'll start by describing some of the most common conditions that are associated with sleep disturbance. Each condition can vary enormously in its severity. So, for example, low mood includes everything from the odd bad day to full-blown clinical depression. Sleep disturbance is one of the first symptoms of any mental distress, so you're likely to notice some disruption if you suffer from any of the conditions that follow.

The worst thing about the relationship between mental distress and sleep disturbance is that a vicious circle is created. That is, the less sleep you get, the harder it is to be logical and to find ways to solve your problems. This makes you more distressed, and hence more likely to suffer from further sleep disruption. That's why it's so important to sort out any sleep disturbance as soon as you can.

Normal sleeping patterns

Before we start talking about what may disrupt your sleep, it's important that I describe a normal sleeping pattern, and the variations that can exist without any distress or disruption. Simply knowing that some variation is perfectly normal will, I hope, prevent you from worrying unnecessarily.

Most adults sleep between seven and nine hours a night, although some people need as little as four hours. You need more sleep when you are younger; so, for example, a baby will sleep for about 16 hours a day, a school-age child around ten hours and someone over 70 only six hours or less.

Sleep occurs in cycles, rather than in one long stretch, and it's normal to wake up briefly between cycles, although you don't usually remember doing so. Each sleep cycle is about one-and-a-half to two hours long, and the length of your own sleep cycle will remain remarkably consistent throughout your lifetime. Knowing the length of your own sleep cycle can be quite valuable when it comes to making up for lost sleep, so I'll show you how to find this out later in this chapter.

Conditions associated with sleep disturbance

Physical discomfort

There are a number of physical conditions that can disrupt your sleep: temporary discomforts such as indigestion or a tickly cough, as well as more persistent conditions such as hot flushes during the menopause, or restless-leg syndrome. Sleep apnoea is another, often chronic, condition that disrupts sleep. In sleep apnoea, the large airways in your body contract as you fall asleep, causing you to wake suddenly.

Chronic pain, particularly back pain, is also a very common cause of sleep disturbance. A particularly cruel aspect of chronic pain is that it's often intensified by particular movements, and sufferers frequently make those movements as soon as they relax enough to fall asleep.

If you suffer from any of these conditions, see your GP. I'll be making some suggestions that can help take your mind off any remaining discomfort, so that you have a better chance of sleeping well even when you're not as pain free as you'd wish to be.

Stimulants and medications

Too much alcohol, caffeine or nicotine can overstimulate your body, and this in turn disturbs your sleep. Remember that caffeine isn't found only in coffee and tea. Chocolate, some colas and sports drinks also contain caffeine. A number of medications and drugs can also disturb your sleep. These include painkillers (they may also contain caffeine), some slimming tablets, decongestants and antidepressants, steroids, beta blockers and street drugs such as Ecstacy and amphetamines.

Anxiety

Sleep disturbance and anxiety, the two most disruptive factors in confused thinking, go hand in hand. The generally anxious – that is, people who worry a lot about all sorts of things – are most likely to suffer from sleep disturbance. However, they're by no means the only ones. Those who are afraid of something specific (phobics) and those who find themselves under stress for a relatively short time, for example students during exam time, also suffer interrupted sleep.

It's not hard to understand why you can't sleep when you're worried, as any sensation of danger puts your brain on alert. You'll start thinking about all the things you haven't done, or the things that might go wrong, so of course it's almost impossible to relax and let go. And even if you do manage to do so, the slightest unusual sound will probably wake you up again.

Low mood/depression

A disturbance in an individual's sleeping pattern is one of the important symptoms that psychiatrists look for if they suspect that a person may be clinically depressed.

This sleep disturbance can show itself in a number of ways. Some sufferers complain that they simply cannot get off to sleep when they first get into bed. They may therefore put off getting ready for bed or settling down until very late, which, of course, compounds the problem. Others wake up in the early morning or in the middle of the night and find that they can't get back to sleep. Still others report that they toss and turn all night, sleeping so little that they resort to taking long naps during the day. They do this in the belief that it won't matter so much if they don't sleep at night, although what actually happens is that they lose any sense of a regular daily routine, so they're in danger of becoming even more depressed and disorientated. Furthermore, because they've rarely been taught how to nap wisely, they wake from these long naps feeling even more exhausted than they did before they fell asleep. I'll teach you how to nap effectively later in this chapter.

Obsessions and compulsions

Obsessive and compulsive behaviour is an incredibly common condition. What starts as an admirable attempt to 'get organised', or to 'sort things out', or to 'regain control' sometimes slips into rigid, exhausting and often pointless routines. The extreme end of this condition, obsessive-compulsive disorder (OCD), is thoroughly debilitating. Sufferers are plagued by a constant stream of worries that disrupt their attention and concentration. These worries usually take the form of an endless recital on one theme – this is the obsession. The wording or the form of the obsession may vary, but the emotional message usually stays constant. Most often the sufferer is afraid, afraid for his or her own safety or for the safety of a loved one.

An OCD sufferer may discover that he or she can relieve their discomfort by behaving in a particular way – this is the compulsion. The compulsion usually involves checking or cleaning something; for example, checking that the doors of their house are locked or washing their hands a certain number of times a day. Even though they know that what they're doing is irrational, sufferers will still say that they believe their compulsive act is somehow protective. It's true, these compulsive behaviours offer relief, but only temporarily, as the worries soon begin again. The more often the sufferers perform the compulsion that relieves the anxiety, the sooner they feel anxious again. They may start to force themselves to stay awake and alert for longer and longer periods of time so that they can get through their routines 'properly', and this is where sleep disturbance begins.

If you're obsessional, you may lie awake at night running through mental checklists to reassure yourself that all is in order. Some people get out of bed again and again, sometimes dozens of times, to perform the safety behaviour once more, just to make sure they've done it correctly.

These compulsive routines tend to grow in complexity, and the time needed increases to the point where they may take so long to perform that there's not enough time left for the other demands of the day. In particular, there's no longer enough time to rest adequately. To take an extreme example: one of my patients told me that he needed three full hours to shave and wash properly each morning because he had to pause and check each move he made carefully. That meant he had to get up at five in the morning to be ready to leave for work at eight.

Trauma

Sleep disruption is common just after something unexpected happens, particularly if it was unpleasant. The disturbing event may be physical, such as being jostled, then losing your footing and falling in a crowd. Or it may be more psychological, for example, if someone makes a cruel remark to you at work. Either way, you may continue to feel upset for the rest of the day, and then find that you have trouble falling asleep that night.

The extreme end of trauma is known as post-traumatic stress disorder (PTSD). Victims of PTSD have suffered an unexpected and terrible shock, for example as passengers in a car crash or as hostages in a terrorist attack. These individuals are highly likely to find themselves unable to sleep for some time, and when they do manage, many of them will experience nightmares that usually contain flashbacks of the trauma. Sufferers wake from the nightmares feeling extremely distressed, and they don't dare to fall asleep again in case the nightmare recurs. They may force themselves to stay awake for long periods, and this of course compounds their distress because the sleep deprivation makes them feel depressed and disorientated. Mercifully, this acute phase of PTSD is usually time limited, and once the frequency of the flashbacks diminishes, so does the fear of falling asleep.

Attention deficit hyperactivity disorder (ADHD): sufferers and their families

Children with ADHD are highly distractible. They don't seem to be able to maintain attention or to listen carefully, and they can be fidgety, impulsive and constantly on the go.

Sleeplessness is not a defining characteristic of ADHD but most people who try to care for someone with ADHD report that the sufferer appears to need very little sleep. I suspect that most of these sufferers – and most are children – actually do need more rest than they have, but because they never relax, it's hard for them to fall asleep. Instead, they do so only when they're simply too shattered to go on.

Their exhausted carers are unlikely to sleep restfully either, even when the rare opportunity presents itself. They're too used to being on the alert, and they seldom manage to relax enough to let go and fall asleep naturally. One parent told me he feels like a coiled spring, always ready to protect his son from the dangers he seems to invite because of his carelessness and inattention.

The result is that the entire family, not just the child with ADHD, is usually sleep deprived – that's why the title of this section is 'Attention deficit hyperactivity disorder (ADHD): sufferers and their families'. The fact that everyone's tired, not just the child with ADHD, is often overlooked. This is a big mistake, because when carers are exhausted they'll find it difficult to concentrate adequately, and, as a result, they may not be able to benefit from the helpful advice that the doctors and psychologists treating their child may give.

Anticipation

It's extremely common to find that you're unable to sleep if you're about to face a life-changing event. This event can be anything from threatened redundancy to getting married. It's interesting to note that the event is as likely to be one that is wanted or longed for, as it is one that's dreaded.

In both cases the mechanism is the same: your anticipation and your readiness for action create such a state of tension that it's impossible for you to relax, and therefore to drop off to sleep. You may lie awake, literally all night, thinking about the forthcoming event, with your thoughts racing from topic to topic. At least you know that once the event takes place, your normal sleep patterns are likely to return quite quickly. And for those of you who are awaiting a longed-for event, the anticipation and resulting sleeplessness may even seem delicious.

Endurance

There will be times when the outcome of a life-changing event is unknowable until the last minute, or when the stakes are high and the outcome will be determined largely by your skills and strategies. Buying a house, taking final exams and completing a big business deal are good examples.

In these situations, it's not surprising that the tension and anticipation interfere with your ability to sleep. What is surprising, however, is that you'll notice little, if any, distress at the time. But even so, you'll still want to find ways to help yourself sleep more restfully, simply because you won't want your abnormal state of wakefulness to affect your judgement and performance.

Most of you can get away with this for short periods of time. When you're in emergency mode, you can sleep very little without suffering any ill effects. However, should the situation become prolonged (that is, go on for more than two or three weeks without a break), you may start to find that your judgement and your ability to concentrate are affected. It's wise, therefore, to take compensatory action of some sort. Power naps are probably the most effective technique to use, and I'll talk about these later.

Habit

It's important to remember that what started a problem may no longer be what's maintaining it. Many people who have come to see me with sleep difficulties know exactly when and why their problem began. A bout of depression, a parental divorce, or childbirth are all good examples. But because that precipitating event is over now, or no longer relevant, they can't understand why they're still having problems sleeping. There are, of course, many possible explanations, but the most likely is simply that the pattern of poor sleeping has now become established as a firm habit.

Habits maintain themselves. That is, it's easier to go on doing the same thing than it is to learn to do something new, so people will persist with their habits even when they don't like them, or when they know those habits aren't doing them any good. You may therefore need to learn how to break well-established habits. I'll help you understand how to do that, too, later in this chapter.

These, then, are the some of the reasons why your sleep may become troubled. Just as there are many causes for sleeplessness, there are lots of ways to help you to sort it out. It's worth noting that no one I've treated has improved significantly using only one approach. I suggest you try out a number of the suggestions that follow. You can then make up a treatment package, using as many of the ideas as you like.

First steps

Before you try out any of the suggestions that interest you, there are two steps that everyone will need to take first:

1 Keep a baseline sleep diary

If you were to ask three people to describe the same event, you'd get three different descriptions. After all, nobody can remember everything. But the interesting point here is that very often, what you remember has more to do with what you already believe than it does with what's actually happening. So for example, if you believe it's always cold in February, you'll notice the days when it's cold, and forget to notice the warmer days. On the other hand, someone who considers February to be the beginning of spring is more likely to notice the warmer days and to disregard the cold ones.

Although selective remembering makes life easier because that way you don't have to revise your theories and beliefs about the world, it also comes at a cost. If you ignore everything except that which proves what you already believe, you won't notice if your theory or belief becomes outdated. This is why it's absolutely vital to start by verifying whether what you think is happening, actually *is* happening. This applies not only to sleep disturbance, but to any problem that may trouble you, so I'll be repeating this advice throughout the book.

A baseline diary is simply a record of when your problem occurs, what else *is* happening when it occurs, and how you react to its occurrence. The key is that you record what's happening at the time that it actually happens, rather than trying to remember the incident later. Recording the information as it happens, or as soon after as possible, ensures that you generate an accurate picture of your problem.

Here's how you keep a baseline sleep diary:

Make sure there's a clock in your bedroom and place it nearby where it's easy for you to see it. Keep a pen and paper, or a photocopy of the template I've included below, where you can reach it. Then record the following information to establish your baseline data:

1 What time you get into bed.

2 What time you last remember being awake (this needn't be exact – a rough estimate will do).

3 Any times you wake up in the night, together with why

you think you woke up and how long you'd guess you were awake.

4 What time you wake up in the morning.

5 What time you actually get up.

6 How rested you feel when you get up, based on a percentage rating where 0 means you're not rested at all, and 100 means you're totally rested.

It's also helpful, particularly if you wish to discover the length of your sleep cycle, to add up the total time you slept.

Plan to keep this diary for five to eight nights. If your weekdays are very different in character from weekend days, be sure to keep your diary on at least one weekend and one weekday night.

Most of you will be surprised to discover that things aren't quite what you thought. Many of my patients, for example, discover that it takes less time than they thought it would for them to get to sleep. This is because we usually overestimate the amount of time that passes when we're feeling uncomfortable. This information provides you with the first really accurate picture of your problem. It will help you to become aware of any incorrect beliefs that you may have about when and under what conditions you sleep best.

Continue keeping your diary as you try out the suggestions that appeal to you. That way, you can compare your original sleep pattern with your current ones, to discover which techniques work and which don't. And keep all these records somewhere safe, because if you relapse, you then have a tailor-made instruction manual ready.

Baseline sleep diary

Date: Day:

Event	What time	Length of time	Why woke (if relevant)
Into bed			
Fell asleep			
Woke			
Fell asleep again (1)			
Woke			
Fell asleep again (2)			
Woke			
Fell asleep again (3)			
Woke			
Fell asleep again (4)			
Got up			
Total sleep time			

Any general information (why slept well/badly?)	
How rested overall? (%)	
Which suggestions tried? (if relevant)	
How successful? (% optional)	

2 See your GP

Book a double appointment if at all possible, and take your sleep diary so that you can explain clearly and accurately what you think the problem is. Describe the pattern of your sleep disturbance; that is, whether you can't fall asleep at first, whether you wake during the night, or whatever is happening. Let him or her know how long the problem has been going on, when you last slept well and what sleeping well means to you.

Your GP will look for any general physical condition that you may have, or any stimulants or medications you're taking that may be contributing to your sleep problem. They will also be alert to any underlying physical condition that may be causing a sleep disturbance, such as sleep apnoea, anaemia, or inflammatory bowel conditions. It's obviously best to sort these problems out first, before you start dealing with the psychological issues.

In anticipation of any of my suggestions you may decide to try, I suggest that you also ask your GP if there is any sort of physical activity that you should avoid, given your medical history.

If you suspect that part of the problem is that you sleep with someone whose snoring keeps you awake, try to persuade your partner to come with you to your appointment. Persistent snoring needs medical attention in its own right, so again, your GP can help.

For the lucky few of you, attending to the physical problems will take care of your sleep difficulties entirely. However, for most, this step simply clears the way so that you can get started sorting out the psychological issues.

If your GP identifies that psychological problems are causing your sleeplessness, particularly if they consider you to be depressed, you may be offered medication. If you consider taking medication as part of your treatment – and many people do – be sure to ask how long you need to take it and what side effects and contraindications it might have. Your GP can probably also give you some idea of how likely you are to suffer from any of the potential side effects.

However, if you decide to take medication, don't expect that it will solve your sleep problems entirely – or permanently. Medication of this sort generally targets symptoms, but not the causes. To ensure a lasting improvement, particularly once you stop taking the medication, you'll still want to address the conditions, behaviours, and beliefs you hold that may have given rise to your problem and that may be helping to maintain it.

Getting a good night's sleep

Once you've taken these two preliminary steps, you'll be ready to choose what you think might help you get a good night's sleep from the following suggestions:

1 Get to know your sleep cycles

Sleeping is more active than you might realise. A typical adult will sleep for seven to nine hours every night, although the sleep isn't continuous. It consists of cycles, and within each cycle you relax, heal and recover if you've been injured or traumatised, grow if you're young, and dream. Each cycle lasts for about one and a half to two hours. You wake up for about a minute between cycles, but usually you won't remember that you have.

As I said previously, the length of your sleep cycle will remain remarkably consistent throughout your life. What will change, however, is the number of cycles that you'll need each day to feel rested and refreshed. As a general rule, you'll need fewer cycles as you grow older. So for example, a baby is likely to sleep through eight or nine sleep cycles a day, whereas an older adult may get by happily on two or three cycles. You will, however, require more cycles when you're growing or when you're under stress. The need for more sleep when you're stressed is particularly unfortunate, because this is the very time when it's difficult to sleep.

It's important to remember that you'll feel much better if you wake up at the end of one of your sleep cycles than if you wake up somewhere in the middle. That's why you can feel so disorientated if you're wakened by a sudden noise; you were probably in deep sleep and not yet ready to wake up. You can now see how helpful it is to determine the length of your own sleep cycle. That way, for example, you can arrange the time you wake up to coincide with the end of a cycle.

To find your own sleep cycle length, get out the information you gathered in your baseline sleep diary. Subtract the time you woke up from the time you fell asleep each time – there will probably be several of these intervals each night. Next, discount the intervals when you woke up because something disturbed you, such as when your alarm clock went off, or because an unexpected noise woke you.

Now have a look at the remaining intervals: the ones when you woke up naturally, perhaps because you had to go to the loo, or simply when you realised that you were awake. Compare these interval lengths to find a common divisor. You can do this either by taking an average of the figures, or simply looking at them to see what number between 1.5 and 2.5 divides most readily into all of them.

This needn't be exact to work well for you. Say, for example, you came up with the following intervals (in hours): 3, 7.5, 6 and 9. These all divide by 1.5, so your sleep cycle length is probably 1.5 hours. To take a less tidy example, say the figures you obtained were 4, 5.5, 6, 8 and 1.75. The best divisor here is probably 2, so your sleep-cycle length is most likely 2 hours. If that seems unclear (and 5.5 and 1.75 didn't fit exactly, it's true), then keep a baseline for a few more nights. Perhaps 1.75, or one and three quarter hours, will actually fit better. Most people find that their sleep cycle length is between 1.5 and 2 hours.

This is a rather clumsy method, I know. Most of my patients obtain an initial estimate after three or four nights of keeping a baseline sleep diary, and then refine their estimate by waking themselves a few times at what should be the end of a sleep cycle, when they should find it fairly easy to wake up. This rough and ready approach is best, I think, because the only way to obtain a truly accurate figure for your sleep cycle would be to stay in a sleep laboratory overnight where technicians could take brain wave recordings to obtain the necessary, precise information. Such an option isn't open to many of us, and anyway, the figure needn't be exact to be helpful.

You're now in a position to decide the best times for you to go to bed, depending on when you have to get up. Do remember to allow for the time it normally takes you to fall asleep once you're in bed – you'll find that information in your baseline sleep diary. Most of us need between 15 to 25 minutes to fall asleep.

Let's say, for example, that your sleep cycle is two hours, that you need to wake up at 6.30 a.m. for work, and that it takes you about 15 minutes to fall asleep. The best time for you to get into bed would then be 10.15 p.m. or, at a pinch, 00.15 a.m. to ensure that you have between three and four full cycles of sleep.

2 Take time to relax

If you're chronically tired, you're also likely to be chronic-ally tense. It's hard to relax when you're constantly forcing yourself to keep going, and when you're pushing yourself, even though your body is demanding rest. Furthermore, it takes more energy to keep muscles tense than it does to allow them to relax, so by continually pushing yourself when you're tired, you become more exhausted even more quickly.

It's important, therefore, that you set aside a short period of time each day – ten minutes is enough – to encourage a return to a more relaxed state. The body responds well to routine, and your muscles will relax more quickly and easily if they're allowed to do so regularly. You might like to work this relaxation session into your bedtime routine, as this will increase the chances of getting to sleep at night more quickly.

There are a number of enjoyable ways to relax regularly. One of the simplest is to focus on your breathing. Here are two exercises to help you to do this:

Paced breathing

Allow five minutes for this exercise. Turn off your mobile phone and anything else that might interrupt you.

1 Sit or lie down somewhere warm and comfortable.

2 Close your eyes and breathe in through your nose slowly and evenly, saying to yourself: 1,001, 1,002, 1,003, 1,004.

3 Exhale through your mouth, again slowly and evenly, saying to yourself: 1,004, 1,003, 1,002, 1,001.

4 Repeat this 40 times.

You needn't breathe too deeply for this exercise to be effective. The steadiness and slow pace of your breathing is more important.

Deep relaxation exercise

Another simple way to relax is to try this exercise. I've adapted it from the Alexander Technique (see Chapter 8, Resources and Suggested Reading). It encourages your body to rest fully and to release any built-up tension. As with paced breathing, turn off anything that might interrupt you and allow ten to 15 minutes. You might want to set an alarm or ask someone to wake you in case you fall asleep.

1 Lie down on your back on the floor, with your head resting on a firm pillow or other firm surface, about 7 or 8cm. (3in.) off the floor, so that your spine is as straight and lengthened as possible.

2 Bend your knees up comfortably, with your feet flat on the floor and your legs hip-width apart.

3 Let your arms rest comfortably at your sides, or bend them at the elbows and rest your hands on your chest.

4 Close your eyes and start paced breathing. Imagine that you're somewhere warm and sunny. Don't just visualise the scene – imagine the scents and the sounds, and keep breathing slowly and evenly for the next ten minutes. It doesn't matter whether or not you fall asleep.

5 When the time is up, roll on to your side and get up easily and slowly. (Getting up quickly will disturb the relaxed state you've created and may make you feel dizzy.)

6 Allow a minute or two before returning to your normal activities.

7 It's also helpful to drink some water.

Other ways to relax

There are many other ways to relax regularly. Learn some yoga poses and practise these for ten minutes; a qualified yoga teacher (see Chapter 8, Resources and Suggested Reading) can help you to choose the most beneficial poses for you. Or, you might like to consider learning some other mind and body relaxation technique such as the Alexander Technique (see Chapter 8, Resources and Suggested Reading).

If music relaxes you, yet another option is to make a recording of your favourite and most soothing pieces of music. If you prefer, you can buy pre-recorded relaxation tapes or DVDs designed specifically for this purpose. However, most of the people I've worked with have found that it's more beneficial to use music you know and love – melodies that bring to mind happy memories. This is more effective than listening to music that, although pleasant, means very little to you.

Find somewhere quiet to listen to your music. It doesn't seem to make any difference whether you listen through earphones or not; as long as they aren't uncomfortable, feel free to use them. The key is to do your listening and relaxing somewhere where there are few, if any, other interfering sounds.

Whatever method you choose, the important thing is to make this into a routine, an established part of your day. Most of my patients find that the best time to do this is in the late afternoon, just after they've come home from work. This has the added advantage of providing a marker between work time and non-work time.

If you have small children who rush to see you as soon as you arrive home, you might consider taking your relaxation time before you leave work. Ask if there's a quiet room in the building. (If there's not, perhaps you can persuade your company to make one available. This would no doubt benefit others as well.) If you drive to work, you could relax in the car before you leave for home, perhaps by practising paced breathing while listening to some quiet music. Don't, however, fool yourself into thinking you'll relax if you simply put on soothing music to listen to while you're driving home. This may help your mood, but it won't relax you in the way one of the exercises suggested here will do. Relaxing should be done on its own. It's not effective to try combining it with anything that demands vigilance, and particularly not with driving.

If you choose regular relaxation, be sure to try it for at least three weeks before deciding whether it's helping you to sleep better and to feel more rested. The effect of any new habit cannot be judged properly in less than three weeks – and, in fact, it would be even better to allow a month before you judge its effectiveness.

3 Use power naps

Power naps are wonderful. They're one of the most efficient ways possible to make up for lost sleep. Many powerful people, world leaders among them, have used power naps to help them cope with the long days their work demands.

There's no best time to take a power nap, so you can fit it in whenever seems most convenient. For example, mothers of young children might take one when their toddler is napping. If you have a set lunch break at work, you could use some of that time. If you can manage it, a very effective time for a power nap is when you have your 'afternoon dip', if you have one. This is a regular time each afternoon when, for about half an hour, you often feel quite tired. It usually occurs in the

Power nap

1 Choose a quiet and comfortable place where you're not likely to be interrupted.

2 Turn off your phones, computers and any other equipment likely to disturb you. You can lie down as I described in the deep relaxation exercise, or you can lie on a bed, or you can sit somewhere comfortable.

3 Set your watch alarm or ask someone to let you know when 20 minutes have elapsed.

4 All you have to do during this time is to close your eyes and breathe evenly and slowly, just as you do when you practise paced breathing. You needn't necessarily fall asleep – simply let go and relax.

early afternoon, and that is one of the reasons why many continental countries very sensibly allow time for a siesta.

The length of your power nap is critical. Twenty minutes is ideal, but as long as you allow more than ten minutes but less than half an hour, you'll benefit. You need a good ten minutes to unwind and relax properly, but if you sleep for more than 30 minutes you may fall into a deep sleep. If that happens, you'll feel quite disorientated when you try to wake up.

You don't have to take a power nap every day. You can take one whenever you need one, for example to give you a boost after a bad night, or to give yourself some extra rest in anticipation of a late night that's coming up. It's been suggested that a 20-minute power nap during the day is equivalent to one full sleep cycle at night.

One last word about power naps: I've been quite rigid about the length of these naps, but let me qualify that to say that once you're confident you can fall asleep fairly easily at night, you can start to experiment and discover the optimum length for your nap. Just be warned that long naps (more than half an hour) can make your sleep difficulties worse at night. This is because if you sleep overly long during the day, you'll start to lose a sense of daily rhythm, and your body will then have difficulty relaxing into a longer sleep at night.

Reviewing your sleep pattern

It would be helpful to review your sleep pattern regularly, perhaps once every year, to make sure you're still getting the right amount of sleep. Do this by keeping your baseline sleep diary again for one week. Make a note of any power naps you take and rate how alert you feel each day using a 0 to 100 rating scale. You can then decide whether you need to adjust your sleep schedule, or perhaps add a power nap. This sort of regular check is truly worth the effort, because the amount and the pattern of sleep you need will change with time.

4 Establish a bedtime routine

Although our minds love variety, our bodies thrive on routine. If you've raised children, you'll know that they settle down to sleep much more easily if they have an established bedtime routine. What your own routine consists of is for you to decide of course, but here are some ideas:

- **Take a warm bath or shower** It's best if you have the water lukewarm; so resist turning up the heat, and in any event, avoid really hot water. To make it even more relaxing you might try adding a few drops of essential lavender oil to your bath water, or put some on a flannel or sponge when you're in the shower.

- **Have a milky drink** Milk contains tryptophan, which is thought to encourage relaxation. If dairy products don't suit you, try a herb tea, perhaps with some honey.

- **Listen to calming, soothing music** Music that's familiar, particularly if it brings back happy memories, can be very relaxing. Many of my patients have created their own sleep tape by recording their favourite soothing sounds and songs. They then listen to this while they're getting ready for bed. It's a nice idea to make several different versions of your sleep tape so that you have some variety. A home-made recording is generally preferable to one you buy because of the pleasant memories it will evoke, and because you can personalise the pace and variety of the music to suit your own taste.

- **Read a favourite book** Choose an author or a type of litera-ture that you enjoy, but avoid anything too gripping as this may cause you to feel alert. You might prefer to listen to a book read out on tape or on the radio. This is partic-ularly sleep-inducing because it's reminiscent of being read to as a child, so it brings back a sense of security and well-being. Television, however, doesn't work so well. This is because most people don't focus fully when the television is on, and intermittent attention isn't particularly conducive to winding down. There's also some suggestion that the way the images are presented on television, with frequent interruptions and changes of topic, is also less than relaxing.

You may also find it relaxing to do a final gentle exercise to send you off to sleep:

Wind-down exercise

1 Get into bed and make yourself comfortable.

2 Do 50 paced breaths or the deep relaxation exercise (see pages 38–40). This is particularly effective if you've been using either of these techniques to relax earlier in the day.

5 Reorganise your bedroom

If you associate your bedroom with staying miserably awake, it's a good idea to change the look of it as much as you can. This can also help you mark a fresh start, with the implication that if things look different, the result of your efforts will also be different, and this time, more rewarding.

Consider ways to rearrange your furniture. For example, place your pillows at the other end of the bed so that you'll now lie down in the opposite direction. Change the bed cover to give your bed a new look. Change the location of any pictures or posters in your bedroom, or swap them for others that you have hanging elsewhere.

If you can't change or reorder anything already in the bedroom, consider bringing in something new; for example, a vase of fresh flowers or a bowl of lavender pot pourri. Lavender is particularly good because the scent induces a feeling of relaxation.

These sorts of changes may seem trivial to your conscious mind. But when you announce, in this way, that you're ready for something new or that you're about to make a fresh start, you'll be making a powerful suggestion that will boost your motivation, and this will feel very encouraging.

The correct temperature and good ventilation in your

bedroom are also important. Make sure, if you can, that there's some way for fresh air to enter the room. And never mind what temperature you've been told by someone else is best for sleeping – choose whatever suits you.

Finally, ensure that your mattress is the most comfortable one that you can afford. If you know you could do with a better mattress, but you can't afford one right now, try turning the one you have around (or turning yourself around on it). Or try turning the mattress over (you may need some help to do this). These changes also suggest that you're making a new start.

6 Break bad habits

If you have some bad habits that you know are preventing you from sleeping well, for example, you eat heavily late at night or you fall asleep in the sitting room watching a television programme, you'll want to get rid of them. Unfortunately, such habits are comforting, and so they won't be easy to eliminate.

The best way to get rid of a bad habit is to replace it with a better one. This avoids you focusing on the bad habit. You also need to practise your new habit at least every night for a month before you can be sure that the new habit is strong enough to replace the old one.

As an example, let's take the tendency to overeat at night, and let's say that what you can't resist are cakes and biscuits. In the morning, before they tempt you later on, throw them out or give them away. Put something that's lighter and easier to digest in exactly the place you previously kept the cakes and biscuits. A banana or an apple are good substitutes. Eat these instead when you feel hungry at night.

If your bad habit is to fall asleep in front of the television, remove the chair or sofa in which you normally fall asleep, or move the television to a room where the seating is less comfortable. Record the programme you normally watch so that you can see it at another time and curl up in bed with a good book instead.

7 Keep a worry book

Many people say that as soon as they settle into bed, or if they wake up at night, they find that their mind starts buzzing. They'll start thinking about all the things they didn't do during the previous day, or they'll focus on anything they did badly, or they'll start to worry about what they'll have to do tomorrow. This is particularly true of individuals with obsessional tendencies, and of those who describe themselves as perfectionists. A worry book is a simple way to prevent thoughts keeping you awake.

Get hold of a notebook. Any type will do – we use school exercise books in my clinic – and keep it by your bedside with a pen or pencil. If your room is extremely dark all night, or if you sleep with a partner who wakes easily, keep a small torch at your bedside as well.

When you wake up and start to worry, write down in your book whatever's bothering you. If you like, you can also make a note of what you can do tomorrow to deal with that worry. If another worry comes to mind, write it down as well. Carry on until no more worries come to mind. (Some people turn their worry book into a 'to do' list.) When no more worries come to mind, tell yourself that you can stop worrying because whatever was troubling you is now written down. You won't forget it and you may even have worked out how to sort it out.

This exercise is very similar to a technique known as focusing, which has been used to clear the mind effectively in preparation for meditation or mindfulness.

Some people prefer to write out their worry list before going into the bedroom to get ready for sleep – and this a good way to start dissociating your worries from the bedroom.

However, even when you do this, you may find that one or two more problems occur to you once you're in bed. Be prepared, therefore, to continue the list. But at least the worry time in bed will be short.

8 Maintain a sensible diet

To help to keep your energy levels consistent and to make it easier to wind down at the end of the day, it's better to eat often and moderately throughout the day than it is to eat a large meal in the evening. Most of you will sleep best if you finish your last meal several hours before you go to bed. Avoid excess alcohol or caffeine with that meal, because they can overstimulate you, and you may then underestimate how tired you really are.

At the other extreme, some people wake up early because they didn't eat enough the night before and are hungry. If you suspect that this may be part of your problem, have a small snack before going to bed, but avoid fatty or sugary foods. Choose a milky drink or a cup of herb tea with honey, a piece of toast or a wholemeal biscuit, or a banana. These foods contain either B vitamins or tryptophan, so they can help you to feel relaxed.

9 Take regular exercise

One of the reasons you're having difficulty sleeping may be that you've not taken enough exercise. We seem to have forgotten that the human body is designed to function best when it has gentle, steady aerobic exercise on a regular basis.

I strongly recommend that you include at least three sessions of aerobic exercise each week as part of your treatment for any sleep disturbance. Talk to your GP about which exercise is best for you. There are many possibilities: walking, jogging, swimming, cycling, and using cardio machines in the gym are a few of the more popular choices. By a session, I mean 20 to 30 minutes of steady movement. Steady movement is more important than great exertion for our purposes, because the aims are to encourage deep breathing and to release endorphins, which, in turn, improve your mood. Regular aerobic exercise is also a key factor in reducing anxiety, so I'll be talking more about it in Chapter 3.

The other thing I would say with regard to exercise is that the timing of your workout is important. Exercising later in the evening may leave you feeling more alert than you'll want to be when you're getting ready for bed. Plan to take your exercise at least several hours before you go to bed.

The benefits of regular exercise are not always immediate, so do be patient. It generally takes about six weeks before you'll notice how much more relaxed you're beginning to feel at bedtime.

10 Be a 'good parent' to yourself

If you're one of those people who can't get to sleep even though you're feeling really tired, and even though you're not feeling particularly worried, then you may find this suggestion particularly helpful.

Prepare a retreat for yourself. Choosing a room where you feel really comfortable. You'll need a comfortable chair and a small table or similar surface. Keep a blanket or duvet in the room, and perhaps a small heater if you feel the cold easily. Remember that it may be quite cool in the middle of the night, and you'll want to be comfortable. You might even include a hot water bottle and a ready-filled kettle.

Keep a notebook and pen on the table so that you have another worry book – or you can use the notebook as a diary if you prefer. Make sure there's a selection of books or magazines in your retreat. These should contain the sort of material you've always meant to read, but that you never got around to reading. You'll want this material to interest you some-what, but on the other hand, it shouldn't be so fascinating that it might wake you up even more. Include a ready-filled kettle, if you haven't already, and a mug and spoon, your favourite herb tea or other non-caffeine drink, and perhaps a jar of honey.

You can add anything else to the room that you feel would make the retreat seem welcoming: a radio, or your relaxing music tape, or a story tape with tape player or iPod. You could add a bowl of potpourri and a bottle of lavender or other calming oil. The overall aim is to make this place as cosy and as inviting as possible – relaxing and soothing, but not too interesting. Make sure that everything you might want is already in place, so that once you go to the retreat you can stay there comfortably.

Then if you can't sleep at night, and you've already tried the relaxation exercises, get out of bed and go to your retreat. This is preferable to lying awake unhappily in bed for long periods of time, because it stops you from associating your bed and bedroom with an inability to sleep.

Once in your retreat, settle into the chair and make sure you're warm enough. Make a cup of herb tea, or prepare your hot water bottle. If any worries have occurred to you since you got out of bed, write them in the worry book. You might read one of the books or magazines, or listen to the radio or your music tape. Stay until you start to feel sleepy, at which time you can return to your bedroom. Imagine that you take the feeling of relaxation you've created with you back to your bedroom. Once you're in bed again, close your eyes and concentrate on your breathing, or on the feelings of warmth and relaxation you've created.

If you're still awake after another half an hour (and don't worry if you are – remember, bad habits don't disappear suddenly), simply get up and go back to your retreat and occupy yourself as before, until, once again, you start to feel sleepy. Repeat this sequence as often as necessary, and tell yourself that when you actually, truly need to sleep, you will.

The key to making the retreat work for you is your attitude. Don't think of it as a punishment. Rather, tell yourself that your body will sleep when it really needs to, but that in the meantime you're going to use your time constructively and enjoyably.

What you're doing here, in effect, is parenting yourself well. A wise and kind parent would take exactly this line with a child who wasn't able to sleep. A wise parent would never scold that anxious child, nor tell him or her what a failure they were for not sleeping. Instead, the parent would distract the child with unexciting but comforting activities. This would enable the child to relax and fall asleep. You'll be doing just the same for yourself.

For the first few nights you may find that all this getting up and going back to bed makes you feel more tired, not less. But because you're eliminating self-criticism, and because you're providing yourself with an environment where you can feel safe and comfortable, you'll soon start to relax and to fall asleep. Eventually, if you wake up at night, you'll find that simply knowing that there's a comfortable place waiting for you if you need it will be enough to reassure you, and you'll fall asleep again without getting out of bed at all.

CASE STUDY: **Rose**

At 76, Rose was one of the oldest patients referred to me. She'd made an appointment to see her GP because she'd been feeling increasingly tired and confused, and was concerned that there might be something seriously wrong with her. Her GP referred her to the gerontology department at the local hospital, but, thankfully, the tests and interviews ruled out either dementia or depression.

However, Rose continued to feel ever more tired. She complained of being unable to sleep at all for more than half an hour at a time. Her GP therefore suggested that she try a course of cognitive-behaviour therapy. Rose had been extremely sceptical about the value of psychological treatment, but her GP had been adamant, so she'd reluctantly agreed to try.

When we first met, Rose told me that she had more or less given up hope of sleeping through the night. She told me that each night she would wait until she felt really tired before she went to bed, hoping that would allow her to fall asleep at once. Even then, she said it seemed a very long time before she fell asleep, and as soon as she heard the slightest sound, she'd wake up again and feel unable to relax or to get back to sleep.

Rose's bungalow was situated near a busy road, and she said she thought that it was the noise of the traffic that woke her most often. She and her husband had moved to their bungalow in town a year ago because they wanted to stay independent for as long as possible. They had decided to move from their village so that they could walk to get everything they needed.

The couple had been married for 51 years and, during most of that time, they'd lived in a cottage in the countryside some 15 miles away. They'd raised their three children there, all of whom now lived some distance away. Rose explained that she and her husband had been happy in the village, and that she'd been sorry to leave. However, since their move they'd met several of their neighbours and had joined a nearby church, so she felt they were beginning to make friends. Nonetheless, she told me that she still felt lonely at times, and that she missed her friends more than she'd realised she would. She said there were times when she regretted the move.

Rose described her marriage as close and supportive

and she asked if her husband could attend the sessions with her. This seemed a good idea. She told me that she'd always been a light sleeper, and it wasn't difficult to discover when and why this had come about. When she was 14, her younger sister had begun to walk in her sleep and their parents had become extremely worried that her sister would come to some harm. In fact, she'd already once walked out of the house and on to a main road. They therefore moved Rose into the bedroom with her sister, and asked her to alert them if she got out of bed. Rose described her parents as 'incredibly strict, you'd never dare to question them', and she quickly learned to wake up immediately at the slightest sound from her sister.

This situation persisted for nearly six years, until Rose married and moved away. She and her husband then settled into their rural cottage, where there was very little noise at night – any sounds were mainly of wildlife. For many years Rose had been woken only two or three times each night, usually to the sound of the occasional traffic, and she'd always been able to settle back to sleep easily. She'd become quite used to, and comfortable with, this pattern even though she said she slept less than she might wish. She'd only begun to feel seriously tired since they'd moved into the bungalow.

After telling me her history, I explained to her the importance of keeping a baseline sleep diary so that we could have the most accurate picture possible of her difficulties. Rose agreed to keep her diary for two weeks.

She did this, and the information in the diary was quite sobering. It took her on average 70 minutes to fall asleep the first time each night. She would then wake up about five times each night, and sometimes it was as often as eight times. It took her between half an hour and an hour to fall asleep again each time. Overall, Rose was getting only about four hours of sleep each night – no wonder she felt tired! Her diary showed that it was the sound of traffic that usually woke her, although she also woke if there were any sudden or unusual noises. However, her husband commented that she didn't stir if the local owl hooted or if a dog barked.

It seemed that Rose had two distinct problems relating to her sleeping pattern, and that it would be best to tackle them one at a time. The first problem was her inability to fall asleep when she first got into bed each evening, and the second was the difficulty she had getting back to sleep whenever she woke up during the night.

We began with her inability to get off to sleep initially. Rose told me that she knew she was listening out for traffic, but that she couldn't seem to help it, and that this made her feel tense. She was acutely aware of the slightest noise, and as soon as she heard any traffic noise, she'd start worrying about her inability to sleep generally. I suggested she try earplugs, but she found these were uncomfortable. My next idea was to get her to make a tape of her favourite music.

Unfortunately, rather than masking the noise of the traffic, the music tape seemed to make her feel even more alert. Her husband then suggested they try to find a tape of wildlife sounds, and, not without some difficulty, he managed to find a recording of birdsong.

The result was dramatic. Rose would start playing the birdsong tape and she would be asleep within ten minutes, representing a reduction of about an hour. She said that the sound of the birds singing made her feel like she was back in the village where they'd lived before and where she'd been happiest. Her husband was delighted, and volunteered to stay awake long enough to turn off the tape for her.

Our next problem was to decide what to do when she woke during the night. Rose liked the idea of establishing a retreat. She was more rested now, and she was also beginning to feel more hopeful. In fact, she became quite enthusiastic about creating this retreat. She loved the idea of having some sweet tea on hand, so she supplied herself with a large selection of herbal teas, as well as kettle, mug, spoon and honey. Instead of 'boring books', as she put it, she decided to set out a blank photograph album, together with all the (many) unsorted photographs she'd taken of her life in the village. She said she'd always intended to organise these photographs, and that this would be a useful way to spend her time awake at night. I was concerned that such a purposeful task might wake her up unduly, but, on the other hand, she'd be thinking about happy memories that might help her to relax.

This photograph album idea of hers turned out to be a brilliant inspiration. The photographs of rural life had much the same effect as the birdsong. Rose soon found that she could only sort her photographs for about 15 or 20 minutes before she felt tired enough to return to bed. She'd then fall asleep almost straight away.

After six weeks, Rose's diary showed that she was waking up only once every two or three nights, and the photograph sorting had become a daytime project. She was sleeping for about six hours a night now, and she felt that this was adequate. Both she and her husband commented that 'putting order' to their past had also helped them to feel more of a sense of continuity in relation to their move, and they were feeling much more settled and happier in their lives generally.

How this applies to you

I hope you can see from Rose's efforts just how important it is to adapt my suggestions to make them fit your own circumstances. Had she stuck with keeping only magazines and books in her retreat, Rose wouldn't have relaxed as quickly, nor would she have felt so comfortable as she did when she was sorting the photographs. Neither would she have clarified and ordered her past so well, and, as a result, started feeling truly settled in her new community.

Never forget that you know yourself better than does anyone else. Take the suggestions I make as mere guidelines to get you started. Use them to shape what you do, so that they fit in to your life. Make sure they're convenient to use and interesting enough to keep you motivated as you continue to overcome your difficulties and improve the quality of your life.

3

Anxiety and Panic Attacks

The only thing we have to fear is fear itself.

Franklin D. Roosevelt, Presidential Inaugural
Address, 4 March 1933

If you suffer from anxiety, I doubt that I need to describe the symptoms. The restlessness, palpitations and feelings of breathlessness, the inability to concentrate, sweating and a vague sense of nausea will be all too familiar.

Anxiety is the feeling you experience when you're faced with a threat, and either you don't know what to do, or you feel that you can't do anything. It's often confused with stress, but for my purposes, I'll be defining stress as *that which causes an individual to feel anxious*. The most extreme level of anxiety is a panic attack, when symptoms such as breathlessness, dizziness and palpitations become so overwhelming that you can feel rooted to the spot. You are desperate to escape, yet unable to move at all.

Anxiety is now one of the most frequent complaints heard in GP surgeries, and a common reason given for missing work and school. It goes hand in hand with sleep disturbance, and prolonged anxiety can lead on to depression. It's a serious problem.

You may be surprised to hear that the symptoms of anxiety

are, to some extent, a sign that your physical body and the survival mechanism in your brain are both working well. In prehistoric times, whenever humans sensed danger, the best chance of surviving it was to hide from it or run away from it. Staying to fight was rarely a wise option, because we didn't have much physical protection – no leathery hide, no claws, no fangs or poison stings – nor were we huge and intimidating compared to, say, a woolly mammoth. Therefore, 'RUN!' has been wired into our brain as a primitive survival mechanism. This survival mechanism hasn't changed much, in spite of the fact that the world about us has.

What all this means is that whenever you sense danger, you'll automatically prepare to run away. You'll breathe in lots of oxygen to feed your muscles so that you can run fast, and to feed your brain so you remain alert to danger. You'll sweat because you can run faster when you're cool, and sweat actually cools the body down. You may well feel nauseous to prevent you from eating, because you can run faster when you're not also trying to digest a meal. And that lack of concentration isn't actually a lack of concentration at all. What's happening is that you're focusing almost exclusively on locating danger. You'll only feel unable to concentrate if you attempt to focus on anything else.

You'll notice, by the way, that I keep talking about danger. What if the danger you're focusing on isn't real, doesn't arrive, or isn't even likely to occur? That's when you'll experience anxiety. When you prepare yourself to deal with something and then you don't, or when you don't know what it is you're dealing with, or if you don't know when a threat may become a reality, then you will feel frightened and helpless – and in other words, anxious.

One of my wisest professors once said to me, 'When a danger is real and present, you won't feel afraid.' There will be no time then to realise how you're feeling, as your survival instinct will take over and you'll simply react instinctively.

That doesn't mean, of course, that it's therefore sensible to wait until you're in real trouble before you do anything about threats to your well-being. It's extremely wise to plan ahead and to anticipate how you might deal with, or, even better, prevent danger. This is called problem solving or strategic planning. However, to do this well you need to be calm and rational, rather than anxious and frightened.

Let's also consider what happens when you remain anxious for long periods of time, perhaps even when anxiety becomes your normal state. Under these conditions, you'll be continually overriding your body's cries for recovery, and it's exhausting to remain poised and ready for flight indefinitely. This state won't feel unpleasant as long as the danger is real and present, as I said previously, or at least as long as you're convinced that it is. But as soon as you start to have doubts, you'll start to notice your discomfort. As you become increasingly uncomfortable and tired, you'll find it harder to remain vigilant, and you may well start looking for stimulants such as alcohol, pills or caffeine to keep you going.

But whatever you do to keep yourself going, sooner or later you'll fall into a state of exhaustion. This is often the time when you go down with a cold, or fall ill with flu. Most of us can remember a time like this, perhaps just after some important exams, or just as we set off on holiday after a gruelling stint at work.

If you don't allow yourself to relax and heal in this necessary recovery phase, and instead force yourself to keep going, you're in danger of setting up a chronic state of anxiety. That's when you start using stimulants to keep going, and then, after a time, using something else to calm you down. As a result, you'll sleep poorly, suffer chronic digestive problems, and feel tired and confused. Sound familiar?

If so, take heart. It's possible to leave the bad habits behind, and it's also possible to feel calm and peaceful much of the time.

However, before I make some suggestions to help you allow

that to happen, I want to describe some of the factors that can cause you to feel anxious. I've already described (in Chapter 1) the common factors in our lives today: the avalanche of negative information on offer from the media, the breaking up of communities and personal relationships, the relentless encouragement to have more than we need or can afford, the pressure to stay eternally young, the constant interruptions that kill any sustained train of thought, and so on. These factors impinge on all of us.

There are, in addition, two further factors that affect only some people. People who've experienced either of these factors react particularly strongly when they encounter stress. They are poor early care and trauma.

Poor early care

There's increasing evidence to suggest that the way a baby is cared for and how well his or her early needs are met will have a lifelong impact on them. This was once mere armchair theorising. Recently, however, evidence has been produced from the field of neurochemistry that appears to back up the theory.

The principles involved in setting up our stress reactors are explained beautifully by psychologists Sue Gerhardt and Steve Biddulph, and I refer you to their respective books (see Chapter 8, Resources and Suggested Reading) if you'd like to learn more about neurochemical development. But, to summarise here: it seems that for some individuals the 'stress thermostat' in the brain has been set permanently too high. This appears to be the consequence of extremely inconsistent, highly negligent or frequently distressing responses to the need for care and nurturing during a child's earliest years of life. When there's such poor care, the brain appears to become set to overreact whenever that person encounters a stressful situation.

If you think this may apply to you, there is, however, no need to despair. Although scientists have no sure way as yet of resetting the thermostat, the fact that you're aware of your vulnerability allows you to protect yourself. You'll need to make it a priority to relax regularly, and to identify the stressors in your life. You may need to take on board more of the suggestions in this chapter, and to practise them more often, than will others.

Trauma

A trauma is an injury or a wound; something you consider to be a threat and to which you react defensively. The extent to which a trauma will affect you depends on how severe it actually was and what it meant to you. So for example, having to give a speech in public may feel traumatic to one person, whereas to another it's merely an exciting opportunity.

To some extent, the first factor we looked at (poor early care) can be classified as just another trauma. However, because it only concerns one period of life, and such a vulnerable one at that, I've dealt with it separately. By contrast, trauma can occur at any time, not just in infancy.

At the extreme end of trauma is post-traumatic stress disorder (PTSD). This condition arises when something totally overwhelmingly negative occurs, such as when an individual witnesses the death or violation of another person, or when they endure this kind of injury or violation themselves. People suffering from PTSD are likely to experience repeated nightmares and flashbacks about the event. They feel unable to control their thoughts about what happened, and they may suffer from sleep disturbances, irritability and an inability to concentrate.

Less dramatic, but nonetheless extremely upsetting, is a trauma that sets off a phobia. For example, if someone is bitten by a dog, he or she might then become afraid of all dogs. An individual who's trapped in a lift may then fear all lifts, and perhaps even all enclosed spaces.

People who experience trauma can, and do, recover. However, they usually need professional help to do so, and they may remain more sensitive to stress afterwards. They, like those who endured poor early care, will wish to pay particular attention to the suggestions I make in this chapter.

First steps

As with sleep disturbance, the best way to start combating anxiety more effectively is to take the first steps. Then read through the suggestions to find those that you think can help you most.

1 Keep a baseline anxiety diary

Just as you're unlikely to remember your sleep pattern accurately, you won't know as much as you think about what triggers your anxiety. Therefore, it's important to start by keeping a baseline anxiety diary for one to two weeks, in which you should record when and under what conditions you feel anxious. For your diary, use the template here, or create your own version. Save the information you gather, because you can use it to help you decide which suggestions are most effective for you. You may also wish to refer to this baseline diary if you relapse.

Take your diary with you whenever you can, because the less time that elapses between the stressful event and you recording it, the more accurate will be the information you gather. You'll be recording all of the events that you rate as stressful.

To determine what your anxiety threshold is, bring to mind two incidents which made you feel anxious enough to register your discomfort. You may have felt breathless, dizzy or slightly nauseous, and/or unable to concentrate on what was going on around you. Now assign a rating to each of these events based on a scale of 0 to 100, where 0 means you're totally relaxed and calm and without a care in the world, and 100

Baseline anxiety diary

Date: Day:

Time				
The anxious thought(s)				
Where was I?				
With whom?				
Doing what?				
Any thoughts				
Any other information				
% anxious				
Which suggestions tried? (if relevant)				
How successful were they? (% optional)				

is the worst anxiety (or panic attack) you've ever known.

You've now established your anxiety threshold. When you keep your baseline diary, record all incidents that you rate as being at least as stressful as either of those two incidents. You'll also make a note of what was happening at the time you felt anxious, as well as just before you noticed your distress. This information will help you discover what triggers your anxiety. Look for physical triggers – for example, you just drank a double espresso – as well as psychological triggers – for example, you'd argued with your partner earlier that day. You'll also want to describe the surrounding circumstances at the time you felt anxious: what time it happened, where you were, and who was there with you. This will help you to identify environmental triggers. The more you know about what causes you to feel anxious, the more prepared you will be when you know you'll be exposed to those factors.

2 See your GP

A visit to your GP will establish whether there are any physical conditions that may be contributing to your symptoms of anxiety; for example, a hormone imbalance or a thyroid condition. Your GP can help you treat these. He or she can also explain the role that medication might play in the treatment of your anxiety, and this will help you to decide whether you want to include it as part of your treatment plan.

There are a wide range of medications that ease feelings of anxiety. Some of them are taken only as and when needed, such as drugs like beta blockers (that control heart rhythm and reduce high blood pressure) and anxiolytics (that reduce anxiety). Others, for example most antidepressants, must be taken regularly, and usually for at least three months, making the commitment to a course of antidepressants greater than to the 'as-needed' medications. On the other hand, the relief obtained from antidepressants is more evenly spread throughout the day.

Of course, medication is by no means a necessary part of treating anxiety. Nevertheless, it's sensible to explore the possibility, because obtaining that information will in itself help you to feel that you're starting to take charge of your difficulties. Be sure also to ask your GP what physical exercise (if any) is contraindicated for you so that you'll know what your options can be if you choose to make exercise a part of your treatment plan.

You're now ready to start putting together a programme to help you avoid anxiety, and to deal as effectively as possible with stress. The following suggestions will help you to do this.

1 Paced breathing

I teach this technique to almost everyone I see during our first session. It's extremely effective, it's easy to learn and the results are immediate. So if you dread those overwhelming waves of anxiety, here's something you can learn that will reduce the unpleasant feelings right away.

When you become anxious, the feelings of breathlessness, the palpitations and the other unpleasant symptoms are the result of an imbalance between oxygen and carbon dioxide in your body. As soon as your brain detects the possibility of danger, your response is to fill your body with oxygen in preparation for action. You probably won't have been aware of it, but for five to ten minutes before you began to feel uncomfortable, you will have been hyperventilating. This means that you've been taking your breath in shallowly, and therefore inhaling more oxygen than you'd normally do in relation to the gases you're breathing out. Normal breathing – that is, breathing when you're calm – is slow, measured and even, and you generally inhale through your nose. When you hyperventilate, on the other hand, you inhale quickly and unevenly, usually through your mouth, and you exhale shallowly.

To rid yourself of your unpleasant symptoms, you need to get rid of the excess oxygen and restore the oxygen-carbon dioxide balance. Paced breathing will help you do this:

1 Breathe in through your nose, slowly and evenly, counting to yourself: 1001, 1002, 1003, 1004.

2 Breathe out through your mouth, again slowly and evenly, counting to yourself: 1,004, 1,003, 1,002, 1,001.

3 Do 40 of these breaths.

I suggest you practise this simple exercise twice a day: as soon as you wake up, and then again when you first get into bed at night. It takes about five minutes to complete, so set your alarm early in the morning so you don't have to rush. This will help you to start and end each day in a more positive frame of mind. If you like, you can close your eyes while you're breathing and imagine yourself somewhere warm and beautiful, perhaps on a beach that you know and love.

After you've practised paced breathing for three or four days, it will start to feel quite natural. You can then use it whenever you're feeling anxious, and, as it's not obvious that you're doing anything unusual, you needn't feel self-conscious. And because you don't need any equipment, you can practise it wherever you are.

2 Graded relaxation

The aim of graded relaxation is to put you in the most relaxed state possible. It's helpful in itself for you to realise just how relaxed you can be; after all, you probably know all too well just how tense you can be. Why not sample the other extreme?

The method I've developed borrows heavily from a technique created by Edmund Jacobson in the 1920s (see Chapter 8, Resources and Suggested Reading for his book *Progressive*

Relaxation). It's based on the idea that your muscles can relax more fully if you tense them as much as you possibly can, and then release them. This will also help you to determine which muscles you habitually tense up. For example, if you try to tense your stomach muscles, but find you can't tighten them much further, you'll know that you're already holding those muscles rigidly.

You won't see the results of graded relaxation as quickly as with paced breathing, and neither can you practise it just anywhere. You'll have to plan your practice sessions ahead of time, allowing about 20 minutes for each session. You'll need a comfortable chair with arm rests, preferably in a quiet room that's pleasantly warm. You can wear your usual everyday clothing, but make sure nothing is binding or really tight. Turn off your phones and computers so that you won't be interrupted.

You'll concentrate on nine areas of your body, moving from the tips of your fingers inward to your shoulders, and then from the top of your head down to your toes. You'll focus fully on each of the nine areas in turn, tensing up the muscles in that part of your body, and then releasing them as completely as you can. Don't move to the next muscle group until the muscles you've just focused on feel comfortable and relaxed.

Graded relaxation

1 **Hands and wrists up to the elbows** With your arms resting on the arms of the chair, make two tight fists. They should be so tight that you feel as if you could punch through a brick wall. Release, feeling as though you've just put down two very heavy suitcases that you have been carrying, or that you've just climbed up a rope.

➡

2 Elbows, upper arms and shoulders Resting your elbows on the arms of your chair, push your elbows downwards, feeling the muscles in your upper arms tensing up. Release, letting your elbows fall inwards off the arms of the chair, and allowing your hands to hang at your sides. At the same time, imagine that your head has become weightless and is floating up to the ceiling, and your neck lifting and lengthening to catch up with your head – you'll feel very tall and light.

3 Forehead and eyes Raise your eyebrows to look surprised, feeling the tension like a tight hat band around your head. Release, feeling as if someone has just given you a soft flannel, warm with lavender water, and you've placed it on your forehead just above your eyes. All the lines around your eyes have smoothed away.

4 Eyes, nose and cheeks Screw up your eyes and nose, as if you've just smelled something foul. Release, and imagine that the skin around your eyes and on your cheeks has become totally smooth, heavy and soft.

5 Mouth and jaw Grit your teeth and grin as widely as you can, stretching the corners of your mouth towards your ears. You'll notice that your neck muscles will also tighten. Release, and allow your jaw to sag and feel slack. It will feel as if you've been chewing gum or tough bits of food.

6 Neck Push your chin down towards your chest, and, at the same time, imagine that you're a string puppet and your head is being pulled up straight and high. Release, and feel as if your head has become weightless and is floating up towards the ceiling, your neck is lifting and lengthening to catch up with your head (as in step 2).

7 Chest Inhale steadily through your nose, drawing your shoulders back and imagining that your lungs are inflating like huge balloons. Release, and exhale the air steadily through your mouth, allowing your shoulders to drop down while your head is floating up, as before.

8 Stomach and lower back Tighten your abdominal muscles, as if you're defending yourself from someone threatening to hit your stomach. Release, and imagine you're lowering yourself into a warm, scented bath. Allow the warmth to melt away all your tension.

9 Legs Stretch your legs and imagine that they are growing several inches longer. Point your toes hard, release and allow your legs to drop back to the floor, relaxing your ankles and toes. Feel as if you've just sprinted for the bus, or just finished running a race.

Now put all of this together, as follows:

- With your eyes closed, imagine that drops of magic – drops of liquid sunshine – are placed on the tips of each thumb and each finger.

- Allow the liquid to sink into the centre of yourself, to help you feel warm and relaxed, and to travel through your body, uniting all your relaxed muscles into one warm feeling.

- Let the golden liquid travel from the fingertips into your hands, then up your arms and into the shoulders. The two warm flowing rivers now join up at the back of your neck to travel up over your head, and then down to wash your eyes, cheeks, mouth and neck into a comfortable warmth. Now the warmth travels into your chest and stomach and back, divides into two rivers again, and flows down your legs to give a feeling of relaxation to your knees, calves, ankles and toes.

- Allow the golden warmth to flow out of you, leaving you feeling comfortable and relaxed throughout your body.

Read through this exercise until you can remember the nine steps without having to refer back to this book. Then, you're ready to start practising.

3 Graded relaxation plus imagery

This will help you learn to relax even when you think about something that would normally make you feel anxious, or when you encounter factors that trigger anxiety. You'll need a quiet room with a comfortable chair, and allow about 30 minutes.

Graded relaxation plus imagery

Start by choosing a subject or a situation that normally makes you feel anxious. Condense it into one image, and then put it aside for the moment. Next, take yourself through the graded relaxation exercise (as described above). Once you're comfortable, introduce your chosen anxious thought in the following way:

1 Imagine that you're sitting on top of a hill on a warm summer day. The sky is blue and there's a slight breeze. You can smell the wild flowers and the freshness in the air. Birds are singing.

2 Far down at the bottom of the hill you can see the object or situation that makes you feel anxious. Perhaps it's an animal; perhaps you see yourself in your manager's office and he or she is criticising your work; perhaps you see yourself at a party standing alone while others seem to be in groups. Keep this image small and far away, and continue to remind yourself of your lovely immediate surroundings. Even as you see that tiny scene below, remember the soft breeze and smell the wild flowers.

3 If, while you're imagining this scene, you notice that some part of your body is tensing up, turn your attention briefly to that part of you. Tense those muscles fully, and then release them back to a state of relaxation. Remember to breathe in, evenly and slowly, through your nose and out through your mouth. You may need to repeat this tensing up and releasing exercise several times.

4 When your muscles feel relaxed again, gently turn your attention back to that small scene below you on the hill. Continue observing it until you can do so while remaining fully relaxed.

5 Now release the image and allow the small scene below you to dissolve or swirl away into nothing, leaving you sitting alone on that beautiful hilltop. Remember the warmth, the breeze, the flowers and the birdsong. When you feel ready, slowly open your eyes.

The next time you practise this technique, repeat every step exactly as you did before. This time, however, bring the distressing image a little bit closer; allow it to be a little bit nearer to you. Take your time when you do this, and check regularly to make sure you're feeling fully relaxed, even while you're observing that far-away scene. If you find that you can't relax fully, simply move the image a bit further back down the hill. Remember, you're in charge of this image, it's not in charge of you. Don't dissolve it until you feel fully relaxed while calmly observing it.

Each time you practise this exercise, bring the distressing image a little closer to you mentally, but only proceed at the pace that's right for you. Avoid setting yourself any deadlines or setting any targets. Remember, even imagining your fear while remaining relaxed, however far away you place it in your mind, is progress. Keep bringing the scene closer until you're able to imagine it as if it's right there with you. The final step will be for you to imagine yourself actually in the scene, speaking to the person you once feared, or stroking the dog that once frightened you.

You'll probably begin to notice, in your everyday life, that when this worrying thought occurs to you, or when someone mentions the subject that once distressed you, or even when you find yourself somewhere near the worrying situation, you'll be starting to feel a bit less anxious than you once did. Your practice will pay off, because this pairing of distressing thought with relaxed body state will begin to generalise. That is, it will occur in more situations than just when you're practising – in real life, not just in your imagination.

As you continue to gain confidence, not only will you stop worrying about the possibility of encountering what once you feared, you may even wish to seek it out. If so, take it gently. Never allow your fear to rise above totally manage-able levels.

It's not easy to overcome a well-entrenched fear by your-self. If for any reason this exercise makes you feel more anxious than you did before, or if it causes you to think more often about your worries, or to become tearful, or even if it just leaves you feeling exhausted, simply return to practising the graded relaxation on its own, without bringing in the imagery.

If, however, this exercise appeals to you even though you'd rather not try it on your own, consider having some sessions of cognitive-behaviour therapy. Because you now already know how to relax, you'll have an enormous head start when you work with your therapist.

4 Adequate rest

When you're tired, your emotions are likely to stop you thinking rationally, and you'll find it much harder to avoid feeling anxious. Adequate rest is essential if you want to deal effectively with anxiety, and you should refer to the suggestions that I made in Chapter 2 in order to help you to sleep better and to feel more rested generally.

5 The relaxation–exercise balance

When I first started working as a therapist, I'd often encourage my patients to choose a programme of regular aerobic exercise that suited their current level of fitness, and I'd urge them to begin working out straight away. This is a great idea if you want to boost your levels of general fitness, but it may not reduce anxiety. There are two reasons why this is so.

First, when you exercise moderately, your heart speeds up, you sweat, and you become somewhat breathless. These are the same symptoms that you're likely to experience when you're feeling anxious. This does *not*, of course, mean that getting fit has the same effect on you as does becoming anxious. Nonetheless, if you experience these symptoms during a workout, you may wonder whether you're endangering your health. Even though this is very unlikely, the thought in itself can cause anxiety. If this happens to you,

you'll need first to establish your safe limit for exercise – the advised upper limit to take your heart rate to. Then you'll need to get used to experiencing the symptoms that accompany aerobic exercise – the slight breathlessness, a faster heart rate and so on. That way, you'll learn to disregard your anxious thoughts when you're exercising, and you can then relax and enjoy your workouts and get the most out of them. Your GP can help you establish your recommended maximum heart rate. Ask him also to recommend a therapist to help you overcome any anxiety you may still feel. A cognitive-behaviour therapist would be the professional most suited to helping you, but that would mean engaging in a course of therapy, which may be a greater commitment than you wish to take on. I'm sure there are sports psychologists, health psychologists, and probably life coaches who also have the training necessary to help you.

The second reason why it isn't wise to use exercise alone to reduce anxiety is because it doesn't provide a balanced approach. Exercise sessions are far more effective if they're paired with sessions of relaxation. Without this counterbalance, exercise may simply wind you up further, rather than help to balance you.

Relaxation

Start learning how to feel more balanced by relaxing regularly. You can use the paced breathing or the graded relaxation exercises, or learn about mindfulness. Alternatively, there are any number of other relaxation techniques you could try. The Alexander Technique and meditation are some possibilities that are currently popular. Any exercise that emphasises proper breathing and calm reflection is what you need. Try to practise your chosen method for at least ten minutes every day.

Once you've established the habit of relaxing regularly –

and this will take at least three to four weeks – you can add exercise to your programme. Remember that for our purposes, the main reason you're including fitness sessions is to reduce your anxiety levels, rather than to achieve any particular level of fitness.

Exercise

Aim for three to five sessions of moderate aerobic activity a week, spaced as evenly as you can manage. By moderate, I mean that you should work hard enough to make yourself slightly breathless, and yet still feel able to hold a conversation. By aerobic activity, I mean any steady movement that you enjoy, as enjoyment is the key to ensuring you continue with your workouts. The most convenient aerobic activity is walking, because you need no special equipment, other than a pair of reasonable shoes, and you can do it almost anywhere. Other possibilities include jogging, cycling, swimming and working out on any of the cardio machines at your local gym. Vary your activities if it suits you, or stick to the same activity. It doesn't really matter, as long as you keep it going and you enjoy it.

This balanced approach to fitness is one of the most powerful suggestions in this chapter. Proper breathing, the ability to relax and adequate rest are all built in to your fitness programme. But, be warned, you need to be patient and keep practising if you want to reap the benefits. It will take about six weeks before you'll start to notice any sustained improvements. But once you become aware of the increased stamina you'll have, and the greater sense of calm you'll feel generally, I suspect that you'll be more than motivated to make this technique a regular and lifelong habit.

6 Thought blockers

An excellent way to reduce anxiety is to fill your mind with thoughts that don't make you feel anxious. That way, there's no opportunity to think about what does cause you anxiety, This is the reason why so many people will tell you that they don't feel anxious when they're really busy.

Of course, the most sensible and natural way to keep your mind too occupied to contemplate anxiety is to build as many pleasant activities into your daily routine as possible. However, if you're already in the habit of focusing on what makes you anxious, you'll need some help at first to get used to blocking out anxious thoughts. And, of course, there are times when, despite all good intentions, you still find yourself in anxiety-inducing situations – for example, when you're stuck in a traffic jam, or if you wake up during the night because of a nightmare. Situations such as these particularly call for thought blockers.

A thought blocker is a mental task that demands a moderate amount of mental effort on your part, preferably using both language and images, and is one that's moderately interesting to you. You'll find, no doubt, that the most useful thought blockers are the ones you invent yourself. However, I also suggest several neutral thought blockers to my patients, so that they have a greater choice when they need to use them. Neutral thought blockers are ones that make you do some mental work, but don't make you feel particularly happy or sad.

Neutral thought blockers

- **Colours** Choose a primary colour – red, yellow or blue. Now name every shade of it you can remember.

- **Flowers** Name as many different flowers as you can. If you're a gardener, you could also tell yourself the best month to plant each one.

- **Streets and roads** Name as many streets and roads near where you live as you can.

- **Names** Remember as many girls' names, boys' names or surnames as you can. You might choose one that begins with each letter of the alphabet.

- **Numbers** Count backwards from 500 (or 600 or 700, if you prefer) by threes, or by sevens, or by 13s.

- **Mindfulness** Focus your thoughts on where you are right now and choose one item you can see that's nearby. Now describe it to yourself in the greatest detail you can. For example, if you chose the chair you're sitting on, describe how comfortable it is. What's it made of? What colour(s) is it? Where is it located in the room? How old do you think it is? Are there any flaws in it? Describe each flaw, and so on.

If you speak another language, you can make any of these thought blockers more challenging by describing the subject of the thought blocker in that language.

You can now see, I hope, that thought blockers require you to use your powers of visualisation to see – a colour, a word, or a number – and then to use your powers of language to name it. This minimises the chance that you can call up any anxiety-inducing thoughts, either in word form or in images. There are, of course, many more neutral thought blockers, and now that you understand the idea, I'm sure you can invent more of them yourself.

Personalised thought blockers

To create your own personalised thought blockers, choose a subject that interests you. For example, if you love music, you might bring to mind your favourite pop group or composer. Now name every piece they have composed.

Alternatively, you might like to use this opportunity to learn something new. If you love poetry, for example, you could memorise some poems. Or you could learn something related to one of your hobbies. To give you an example, one of my patients is a keen football supporter. He decided to memorise the names of all the players in his favourite teams, as well as the positions they play.

Another of my patients, a musician, had been referred to me because of a fear of flying. He decided to invent some thought blockers that would help him improve his musical skills, so he chose various pieces he knew already and mentally transposed them into different keys. He used this exercise while he waited for his flight to take off, and he told me he was so occupied that he didn't particularly notice the plane taking off.

Thought blockers that need props

Until now, I've only described portable thought blockers, the sort you can use any time and anywhere because they don't require any equipment. Of course, if you have the relevant item, there are many other possibilities. For example, you could play a musical instrument. You could phone a friend (with a mental rule *not* to talk about your worries), or go for a run, or turn on the radio. The key is to build your thought blockers around your interests, so the thought-blocking activity is more appealing than your anxiety-inducing thoughts.

7 Social support, not reassurance

The support that our friends and loved ones can give us is appreciated by everyone, but it's particularly welcomed by those who are feeling anxious. We all feel safer when we're with people who care about us, and good company helps to distract us from our worries.

On the other hand, social support can also be misused, so be careful. If you rely on others to reassure you and to relieve you of your anxieties, such relief will be only temporary. Research has demonstrated that the more often you seek reassurance from others rather than reassuring yourself, the shorter the interval will become before you'll need to seek reassurance again. Overall, your anxiety will increase rather than diminish.

Enjoy the company of friends and loved ones, and allow your time together to distract you from your worries, but learn to reassure yourself.

8 Reassuring yourself

The first thing I suggest that you do here is to write down as clearly as you can what worries you. Vague worries left to churn around in your mind can be quite distressing – they feel powerful, and they encourage chronic anxiety. But when you identify the source of your anxiety in black and white, it somehow diminishes its strength.

Now challenge your anxious thought – how realistic is your fear? Gather the facts about that fear: look up information on the Internet, or ask anybody you know who's knowledgeable in that field. This allows you to make a realistic assessment of any threat. Next, summarise what you've learned and write it down. And finally, follow this with a new statement about your worry – one that's realistic.

Let's say, for example, that you have a fear of flying. You start by writing this statement: 'I'd love to travel to somewhere exotic, but I'm afraid to fly because the plane might crash.' Now contact a travel agent, or use the Internet to learn about airline safety measures and to gather the accident statistics. Remember, this information must be taken in context, in that you must compare the number of accidents that have occurred with the number of flights that have taken place. You are then in a position to make a comparison between different modes of transport.

If your research leads you to the conclusion that your

anxiety isn't justified, then you could consider booking a flight straight away. Or, as is more common, if you now feel strongly motivated to overcome your fear, you could book some sessions with a good therapist, or contact a self-help group such as TOP UK (Triumph Over Phobias) (See Chapter 8, Resources and Suggested Reading). Your chances of overcoming your anxiety are now much higher.

If, on the other hand, your research leads you to conclude that your concern is justified, then the comparisons you used when you looked at the risks of flying, relative to other forms of transport, suggest that you might wish to explore alternative ways to travel somewhere exotic.

9 Regaining a sense of control over your life

It's not simply what happens to you that determines how endangered and anxious you'll feel. The critical factor is how you deal with what happens to you. For example, I knew two men who were made redundant at the same time. One became depressed and withdrawn, and after a time he also became agoraphobic (that is, he developed an irrational fear of open spaces). The other decided to retrain in a field that paid very little, but which was something that he'd always wanted to do.

Both men faced the same situation. One, however, believed it to be a disaster, whereas the other decided that it offered him the opportunity to do something he'd always wanted to do.

What I hope you can see is that, although you may wish to change some of the circumstances in your life, it's not necessary to change anything outside of yourself in order to feel you've regained some control over your life's direction.

Of course, there are circumstances that make it more difficult to feel that you're in control. Rigid timetables and inflexible hours at work are good examples of anxiety-inducing practices. And there are of course lots of things that you can't change, such as what time the rush hour starts in your area. Such things may create anxious thoughts for you – for example, whether you'll get to work on time.

But that still doesn't mean that these circumstances need to cause you anxiety. Let's say that you have to be at work at 9.00 a.m., and that the rush hour in your area is between 8.00 and 9.00 a.m., and that travelling at that time makes you anxious. What's stopping you from leaving for work early and making yourself a nice cup of coffee when you get there, while everyone else sits in the queues? Even if you're not paid for that extra time when you arrive early, you can use it to relax or to get a head start on the day. The sense of relaxation and calm you'll feel as everyone else rushes in, complaining bitterly about the traffic, is payment enough, isn't it?

Study your baseline anxiety diary. Identify those times and situations when you feel most anxious, and figure out how you can introduce an element of control into them from your own point of view. Never mind how others view those situations.

Some notes on panic attacks

Panic attacks represent the extreme end of anxiety. Because they're so incredibly distressing, I always try to help my patients learn how to avoid them, rather than learning to control them after they occur.

Many people believe that their panic attacks occur out of the blue. They don't. Panic attacks are always triggered by something; something that frightens you or makes you feel vulnerable, even though you may not have realised it. Therefore, for those of you who suffer from panic attacks, it's absolutely essential to keep a baseline diary. You'll probably also wish to write out a short 'autobiography', listing the dates (or at least the time of year) on which any powerful and upsetting events have occurred. If you'll then take the time to do some clever detective work, you can discover your panic triggers.

Panic triggers

Your triggers may be physical. For example, some people are more likely to become panicky if they have a very low blood-sugar level (if this is the case, you need to make sure you eat sensibly and, probably, more often), or if they're exhausted (see Chapter 2 for some suggestions to help you feel less tired).

Alternatively, your triggers may be psychological and very obvious, such as the object of your phobia (for example, a snake), or a sensational story presented out of context (such as a news story about someone who was bitten by a poisonous snake). If this is the case, I suggest you find a therapist to help de-sensitise you to whatever it is that triggers your panic attacks.

On the other hand, the trigger may be psychological but extremely subtle. For example, one of my patients thought she simply panicked randomly whenever she travelled on the Tube. However, after carefully keeping a baseline diary, she discovered that if she'd noticed anyone wearing a green coat who was also travelling on her carriage, she'd panic. It turned out that she'd been raped over a decade ago after being followed from the Tube by a man wearing a green coat. She'd had counselling after the event, and the counselling had helped her with symptoms of PTSD, but she hadn't realised how far her fear had generalised.

Another example of a subtle psychological cue is what's known as the 'anniversary effect'. Many of us will feel distressed, sad, or even panicky on the same day, or at the same time of day, that something distressing had once happened to us. For example, every spring one of my patients became convinced that she had cancer. Year upon year, she would visit her GP repeatedly during the spring and insist that she have numerous tests. When we looked at the autobiography she'd written for me, she realised that her fears had started when her mother was diagnosed with terminal cancer in the spring, eight years previously.

As you can see, it may be extremely difficult to discover what triggers your panic attacks. I often wonder if this is, in part, because panic attacks are so distressing that we blank out of our memory any thoughts just before the panic attack, including a recollection of the traumatic trigger. After all, we know this can happen with major trauma.

You may find that it isn't possible to rid yourself of panic attacks on your own, even if you identify a trigger or an anniversary effect, and this wouldn't be unusual. If that's the case, I recommend that you seek professional help to overcome them. Cognitive-behaviour therapy is the approach that's most often recommended.

CASE STUDY: **Helen**

Helen, a 36-year-old GP, was referred to me to help her to manage her high levels of general anxiety. Her own GP had offered her beta blockers, a medication that targets anxiety but doesn't need to be taken regularly, but Helen was unhappy about the idea of taking any medication. Her GP had therefore suggested that she try cognitive-behaviour therapy.

At the time of her referral, Helen had two young daughters of four and seven, and she was running her own practice, a popular surgery that had its full quota of patients. Her husband worked in finance and was often away on business.

Helen had been raised in a family that had extremely high expectations. She told me that she'd grown up with parents who simply assumed you'd give your utmost at all times. She described both herself and her mother as 'perfectionists', particularly with regard to appearance. She said that her mother was 'obsessed' about hiding any signs of ageing. Helen had attended local schools and achieved excellent results in her exams, and had gone straight from school to university to study medicine. She said she used to take pride in staying up with the latest medical breakthroughs, but that of late this had seemed too daunting a task. She told me that she felt 'haunted' by the stacks of medical journals, still unread, in her study at home.

Both Helen's parents were GPs, and although her father was well beyond retirement age, he, like his younger wife, was still working full time. She had one younger brother, a consultant neurologist.

During our first session, Helen told me that for her, the inability to fall asleep was the single most distressing aspect of her anxiety. She said that she dreaded getting into bed because she knew she'd immediately start worrying about how long it was going to take her to get to sleep, and of all the things she had to do the next day. These anxieties didn't plague her so much when she was busy, she told me, and so she always tried to keep herself fully occupied during the day.

We decided, therefore, to start with her inability to sleep. She agreed to keep a sleep diary, and also to rate her level of anxiety when she first got into bed. After two weeks, Helen came back to see me. Her sleep diary revealed that it took her over an hour to fall asleep each night. She was kept awake worrying about everything she had to do the next day. Her anxiety rating at bedtime was between 70 and 85 on a scale of 0 to 100.

I introduced to Helen some possible ways to deal with her anxiety at bedtime. She liked the idea of writing a worry book, and agreed to keep one by her bedside. She planned to write down everything she felt she needed to do the next day, and sometimes, when and how she planned to do it.

When she returned two weeks later, Helen said she was feeling a bit more rested. Typically, she'd spend 20 minutes writing in the worry book, and then fall asleep. This represented a reduction of half an hour of time lying awake in bed before she could fall asleep. Furthermore, her anxiety rating when she first got into bed had decreased to 40.

Helen told me that her list of things to do, now that she could see it in black and white, showed her just how much she was demanding of herself. I suggested that she start putting her list of things to do the next day in order of importance, and not to demand too much of herself by expecting that she complete all of them. She felt very pleased about this, and told me that it felt like she was beginning to have more control over her life. She'd begun to accept that her anxieties sprang from her own demands on herself, rather than from those made by anyone else. She'd also become aware that she didn't know how to relax, and she felt that the next step was for her to learn to use paced breathing and the graded relaxation exercise.

When Helen returned for her next session, she was extremely pleased with herself. She told me that it had taken over a week before she was able to release her tension during a graded relaxation session, but that now that she could do so, she noticed that her anxieties were, as she put it, 'more quiet'. She was also using paced breathing at work whenever she began to fall behind in any of the tasks she'd set for herself.

We felt it was now time to introduce some physical exercise into her life, and we decided to combine this with her desire to spend more time with her children. For homework, Helen agreed that she and her husband would plan some sort of family outing each weekend – one that was based on exercise.

At our next session, Helen told me that the family outings were proving to be a great success. They'd taken several cycle rides and one long walk, each time with a picnic. She added that she'd also noticed that she was no longer breathless when taking the stairs at work, and that she felt fitter generally. The exercise was also helping her to sleep more restfully, and her anxiety rating when she got into bed was now down to 15.

Helen needed to adapt and make use of a number of techniques before she began to feel truly able to master her anxiety. This isn't unusual. Perhaps what is a little unusual, however, was her ability to know immediately which aspect of the anxiety to tackle first, which second, and so on.

How this applies to you

You, too, will know which aspect of your problem needs attention first, and which ones can wait, if you'll trust your instinct. If, however, you feel uncertain, then choose the aspect that seems easiest for you to overcome, and work on it first. After all, the suggestions you'll incorporate into your life can only help you, and, in the long run, it won't matter which problem you started with as long as, in the end, you feel on top of things. The important thing is to get started.

Make a point of reviewing your progress every three weeks (remember, that's how long it takes to break a habit). If you feel you've sorted out your difficulties, all well and good. If not, do as Helen did: add another suggestion, and later another, until you feel that you no longer have a problem.

4

An Unhappy Past

The Moving Finger writes; and, having writ,
Moves on: nor all your Piety nor Wit
Shall lure it back to cancel half a Line,
Nor all your Tears wash out a Word of it.

The Rubáiyát of Omar Khayyám
Edward Fitzgerald

The tone and the direction that a course of therapy takes will be greatly influenced by the therapist's first question. If I start a session with a new patient by asking him or her about the difficult times they remember from their childhood, we'll probably spend our time working to overcome their weaknesses and vulnerabilities, and only later, if indeed we have the opportunity to do it at all, will we look at their strengths. If, on the other hand, I start the interview by asking them to recount some of the happiest and proudest moments of their childhood, we're likely to start with their strengths, building on what they already have, even though it may have been masked or forgotten. Thus, two very different courses of therapy are possible, even when the patient, the childhood in question and the therapist are the same.

A course of therapy can either focus on the damage that's

been done, or it can work to build on the good that remains. I much prefer the latter, as it saves so much time and so many tears. It also ensures that you cope better now with whatever happened, and however you reacted, in the past.

Understanding your past

Of course, many of you will wish to discover how and why your pain and your maladaptive patterns started. It can be incredibly reassuring to realise that these patterns weren't always there and that there was a time when they weren't part of you. Such understanding can also help you to avoid repeating the patterns that cause you distress. But this know-ledge can only aim at understanding and only suggest what you might avoid. It's unlikely to help you learn how to behave more adaptively now, at least not directly. Understanding alone rarely changes well-entrenched thinking patterns and behaviours.

Others of you know only too well the origins of your pain and distress. You may wonder how you can ever stop feeling hurt and angry at those who neglected or mistreated you.

If you do wish to understand more about how you came to acquire your problems, or if you want to explore in depth the negative feelings you have with regard to your past, then I'll not discourage you. To do this, you'll need to consider in detail the events of your childhood. This process is likely to be traumatic and difficult, and I therefore urge you to work with a professional. Ask your GP to recommend a good psychodynamic or cognitive-analytic therapist.

However, if you do choose this course of action, I recommend that you do so only after you've made the positive changes I'm suggesting throughout this book. If you start by making improvements in your life as it is now, you can then approach your past with more confidence. You can look at what happened without fearing that it's likely to overwhelm you, because you'll know that you've learned how to deal with anxiety, panicky feelings and negative thinking.

But whether you explore your past in detail or not, I'd urge you to remember that as long as you focus on your negative feelings, even when it's understandable to feel this way, you're allowing your persecutors to continue to direct the course of your life. Only when you've let go of your negative feelings will you be in charge of your own life direction.

Techniques to help you let go

I'd like to help you let go of an unhappy past. You may find this difficult, even when the will is there. I'm therefore going to suggest some specific techniques that can make it easier to do so.

1 Write a letter

This technique is particularly useful if your negative feelings are directed towards someone who may still be in your life. After you use this technique, you'll feel calmer and more able to focus on the present when you're with that person because you will have dealt with the past.

Say that one of your parents was consistently cold towards you, or ignored one of your needs, or in some other way hurt, offended or restricted you. Write a letter to him or her cataloguing clearly, and in as much detail as you can, exactly what upset you. Don't hold back. Be as forthright in your anger as you wish. Sign the letter and put it in an envelope, as if you intend to post it.

Do *not*, however, send the letter. The next step is to destroy it. You can tear it into tiny pieces, or you can burn it, or whatever you wish. Just make sure you destroy it totally. The act of destroying the letter is itself a sort of release. It's as if you're tearing up your negativity, or twisting it into shreds, or permanently deleting it. Doing this also means that there won't be anything left that could inadvertently hurt someone.

When you write a letter, you can unload your anger or pain and clarify why what happened to you was so damaging. Yet you've not actually affected your relationship with the person in question in a way you might regret. The person who hurt you hasn't been hurt by you in return, nor has he or she gained any sense of satisfaction in knowing that they hurt you, if that's what they had intended. You can continue to see them if it's still necessary that you do so. But you can now do so with that weight off your mind; you've said what you needed to say.

Surprisingly often, this technique goes hand in hand with the next one.

2 Do a salvage operation

I'm sure you've heard the clichés about this one already, such sayings as: 'out of adversity comes strength' or 'what doesn't kill you makes you stronger' or even 'every cloud has a silver lining'. This technique helps you take the good from what happened in the past.

What you need to do now is to turn the way you've always looked at your early experience upside down and consider the good that person has done you. 'The *good* he's done me!' I can hear you saying. 'He only hurt me! He only made my life miserable!' But remember this: when we've been wounded, we have a scar. That scar may not be beautiful, but it's strong. In fact, it's even stronger than the surrounding skin. What this means is that you're actually stronger than you were before you were hurt, or were made to endure such misery.

The best way to recognise what you've gained is to use mirror talk. This is a technique I'll talk more about in Chapter 5; but in essence, this is what you do:

Mirror talk

Look at yourself in the mirror and say something like this: 'X did his worst to me. It was totally unfair and I didn't deserve it. But I got through. I survived that unfair, undeserved abuse, and I'm still here. And I'm stronger than ever now.'

If you prefer, you can write another letter instead. Thank whoever hurt you for the strength they've given you, and for the lessons they taught you in how *not* to treat other people. Vow to be an even better person than you would have been if you'd not had to endure this oppression. As before, don't send the letter. Instead, reread it several times and then destroy it. You've reaped the benefits simply by writing down how you've turned a bad experience to your advantage.

Recognise, too, that you're in good company. Take time to read about some of the high-flyers and the great achievers in any field that interests you. You'll find that a large proportion of them endured some great loss, mistreatment or pain, and that they recovered from that experience with an even greater determination to make a success of their lives. You can do just the same.

3 Honey, I shrunk my tormentor

A number of my patients have told me how much they enjoy using this technique, so I'll include it, even though it's not as effective in healing as the other two. I do have to agree, however, that it's good fun to use.

Call a picture up in your mind of the person who hurt you. Clarify the image and make it as realistic as you can. Now imagine him or her starting to shrink. If you've ever watched the film *The Wizard of Oz*, and can recall the scene where the Wicked Witch of the East shrinks into nothing when Dorothy throws the bucket of water over her, then you'll know what I mean. You can either allow your tormentor to shrink into nothing, or you can leave him or her when they're tiny. Imagine looking down at this tiny figure ranting and raving, totally powerless to harm you in any way.

There are many variations on this technique. You can imagine your oppressor in a clown costume, or wearing a silly hat. Feel free to laugh; laughter releases tension in much the same way as does crying, but it's a more enjoyable experience. The release means that your tormentor is losing the power that he or she once held over you. After all, who can be afraid of someone in a clown suit who's only two centimetres tall?

CASE STUDY: Nicky

Nicky was 28 when she first came to see me. She'd previously made an appointment to see her GP because she was having palpitations and dizzy spells, and she thought there might be some problem with her contraceptive pill. Her GP had arranged for a number of tests, and when he was satisfied that there were no physical problems, he asked Nicky if there was any reason why she might be feeling stressed. To her own surprise, as well as that of her GP, Nicky burst into tears. She admitted that she'd been feeling less and less able to cope at work, and she now recognised that she'd been having panic attacks. Her GP suggested that she might consider having some cognitive-behaviour therapy.

Nicky's childhood had not been easy. Her father had moved out when she was a baby, leaving Nicky's mother to raise her and her older brother alone and without any financial help. Her mother was, and remained, very bitter about what she referred to as 'the desertion', and she'd continually lectured her children about the need to 'amount to something instead of being saddled with kids'. Her brother had run away from home when he was 16, and neither Nicky nor her mother knew where he was. Nicky had grown up anxiously trying please her unhappy mother.

At her mother's insistence, she'd reluctantly stayed on at school to take her A levels. When she got very poor results, her mother made her disappointment clear. Defiant for the first time in her life, Nicky left home and moved into a flat with some school friends. She found a job as a shop-floor assistant in the fashion department of a large high-street store. Nicky loved her job and the freedom she began to feel. She told me it was the happiest time she'd ever known.

When she was 22, Nicky met David, who was eight years older than she was. She told me the attraction had been instant, describing David as warm and caring. They'd been together for a year when Nicky discovered she was pregnant. Although she knew she wanted children, she hadn't wanted to become pregnant so soon. Nonetheless, she and David decided to marry and they agreed that Nicky would continue with the pregnancy. Daisy, a healthy and lively baby girl, was born on time and both parents were delighted.

Nicky's mother, however, was furious. She said Nicky was now likely to waste her life, and mother and daughter stopped seeing or speaking to one another. But, with David's encouragement and support, Nicky continued to work for three days a week. Daisy went to a child minder and seemed happy to be there.

Nicky's problems had begun three months before she went to see her GP, when she'd been promoted to the position of manager in her department. Nicky hadn't asked for promotion – she'd been approached by the store manager. She was extremely flattered, but at the same time she was concerned about the increase in the number of hours that the new position demanded. However, her friends and her husband encouraged her to take up the offer. They pointed out that the increased salary would allow her to afford 'so much more'. Nicky accepted the manager's offer.

The promotion meant that she no longer did any of the direct selling that she'd loved, and it also meant that she'd begun working full time. She stopped taking her daily walks and attending a weekly coffee morning with other mothers. It was at that point that she started having panic attacks.

Initially, I saw Nicky for eight sessions. She learned how to control her panicky feelings using paced breathing, and we used graded relaxation and imagery to help her feel more effective at work.

However, during our work together, Nicky had come to realise that she'd prioritised her work more to please others than to please herself. She told me that what she actually wanted was to be at home with her daughter as a full-time mum. She began to feel huge resentment and anger towards her mother in particular, who'd always said she would 'amount to nothing' unless she had a high-paying, high-status job. I suggested to Nicky that she write her mother a letter and tell her how she felt. Nicky enjoyed this exercise enormously, and she also tried the shrinking technique with great enthusiasm and continued to use it for some time.

She and her husband decided at this point to do some careful budgeting to see if they could manage on his salary alone, and they decided that this was possible. Jubilant, Nicky quit work, and it was at about this time that we stopped meeting.

Nearly a year later, I had a call from Nicky. She asked if she could see me again as she had a confession she wanted to make. She told me that about three months after she'd stopped work, she'd begun to feel restless and bored. By the end of six months, she said she was 'crawling up the walls'. Although she loved Daisy more than ever, she'd realised that full-time mothering didn't suit her.

Luckily, because she was such an excellent employee, her company was only too happy to take her back. They'd agreed a 20-hour week and, two months ago, Nicky had gone back to work. She told me that she'd felt much better almost immediately. She'd been pleased to find that Daisy had adjusted to the changes quickly and happily. Initially she'd had some panicky feelings but she'd used the paced breathing and her anxiety had never developed into panic attacks. She added that the anxious feelings only occurred during the first three weeks back at work.

Another reason that she'd come to see me again, Nicky told me, was that she now felt that her mother had been partially right in what she'd taught her, yet she hated to admit it. How could she deal with such ambivalent feelings?

Nicky realised straight away that she'd been thinking in black-and-white terms. She'd simply assumed that her mother was wrong and that she, Nicky, was right. Now she could see that each of them was partially right. After all, it was part-time work that suited her, not working instead of mothering. She also recognised that she did love her work and the sense of achievement she felt when she was there.

I suggested to Nicky that she write a letter and tell her mother what she'd realised, and tell her also how much she now appreciated that her mother had encouraged her to develop more than one interest in her life. Although she said it wouldn't be easy to admit that her mother had been even partially right, Nicky agreed to write the letter.

She came back to see me again a month later. She was elated. After writing the letter, she'd decided to visit her mother, whom she'd avoided seeing or even speaking to for over a year. She wanted to thank her in person for what she'd always previously considered to be her selfish and controlling behaviour. Her mother, usually critical and defensive towards her daughter, had been astonished when Nicky turned up, and at what Nicky had to say. 'She didn't say anything, and that's a new one for her,' Nicky told me. 'She just burst into tears.'

Mother and daughter had then spent the most enjoyable afternoon together that Nicky said she could ever remember. They were now in regular contact again, and to both Nicky's and her mother's surprise, her mother was also proving to be an excellent and loving grandmother for Daisy.

How this applies to you

I'm going to say it once more, because it's so important. There's no need to uncover your past in order to live more productively and more contentedly now. However, if you, like many others, would like to know more about your early life, make sure you're feeling strong and self-confident first. Then, if you do uncover pain in your past, allow it work for you rather than against you.

5

Negative Thinking

There is nothing either good or bad, but thinking makes it so.

Hamlet, II. ii

A large tree that dominated a couple's front garden is toppled by high winds. Luckily no one is hurt, but the man living in the house is distraught. He'd planted the tree, which was a rare variety, over 40 years ago when he and his wife first moved into the house. He had nurtured it tenderly, and, for him, it had been the centrepiece of their garden. His wife, on the other hand, is delighted. The tree had blocked her view of the hills to the west of their village. Now when she sits in their front room she can enjoy the view.

The same event, but with two completely different reactions to it.

How you react to the world

This story illustrates the key issue in this chapter: you may not be in a position to change a great deal in your world, but you're totally free to choose how to react to that world. You can either look for what's good in your life and how you can benefit from your circumstances, or you can feel upset and disadvantaged as a result of what's happening around you.

Your reaction to any event is actually far more complex than it seems. Your senses register the event, of course, but then you make it your own. You decide what happened and why (your logical reaction), and you also make a decision about how you feel about it (your emotional reaction). For example, your young son pushes his sister and she cries. How do you make sense of that moment? Did she provoke him, or is he bullying her? And what's your emotional reaction? Do you feel anger towards your daughter who may have provoked your son, or towards your son who maybe bullied your daughter, or towards neither because that's just kids? As you can see, no one registers a pure objective truth. Each of you will interpret what happens in your own way, and the filters you use are at least as important as the raw material you filter.

Not only do you make a series of judgements about what happens before you encode an event into your memory, but you also decide what to attend to and what to ignore. The world is so rich and there's so much going on all the time that you couldn't possibly attend equally to everything. You are always making choices, and these choices are influenced by your current mood, your history, your interests and whatever else is competing for your attention at any given moment.

Let me give you an example. My husband is an architect and we recently went out for a meal at a restaurant that neither of us had been to before. Later, I asked him what he thought about the people at the table next to us. Did he think they were having an affair? He didn't remember them, but he asked me if I'd noticed that the cornices in the dining room weren't authentic. I couldn't even remember that there were any cornices. Even though we'd spent the same time in the same place, what we each remembered about that evening was completely different.

We're born into a world of exciting sensations and images, but nothing makes sense to us at first. Gradually we learn to separate the world into 'me/not me', then into 'yours/mine', 'familiar/strange' and so on, creating countless classifications depending upon our own particular experiences. We come to know the world through what happens to us, and through what we're told about it. And as we come to know that world, we begin to make predictions about it. We decide what to pay attention to and what to ignore, what to look forward to and what to dread. Parents play an incredibly important role in helping us to shape our world, as later will our teachers, our peers, the media and society at large.

As I explained in Chapter 1, some of the most powerful forces in our society today, the media and advertisers, encourage us to feel dissatisfied with what we have and how we look, to worry about our safety, and to focus on what's going wrong. This way of looking at the world encourages negative thinking.

However, you don't have to think negatively. One of the most exciting and hopeful things I've learned from observing human beings as they develop is that our view of the world is an ever-changing, ever-maturing part of us. If you hold self-defeating ways of looking at the world, you don't have to feel stuck with them. You can modify your beliefs and change your attitudes. In this chapter I'm going to challenge you to do just that.

Common negative beliefs

First, however, let's take a look at some of the most common negative beliefs that are around today. Read each of these carefully, and try to identify which ones you use to reinforce any negative thoughts and feelings that you may have.

1 The problem's not me, it's out there

This is also known as external attribution, or blaming your environment for your own unhappiness. 'If only my husband wasn't such a stay-at-home, I wouldn't be agoraphobic.' 'If only my daughter was easier to handle, I'd be able to work full time.' Nonsense. Blaming others for your own problems not only makes it seem as if there's no way out, but it will also eat away at your self-confidence.

You shouldn't expect to change other people. Their point of view will be different to your own, and, anyway, they won't see life's difficulties in the same way that you do. Any changes you make should start from within you, with your view of your own abilities and your interpretation of what's going on around you.

Remember, however, that taking responsibility isn't the same as feeling guilty. Guilt wastes your energy, because you're feeling bad about your past, and the past can't be changed. Why not use that energy to make things happen now?

2 I feel threatened

In Chapter 1, I talked about the inaccurate picture of our world that the media paints. If you read the newspapers and watch the news, you'd think we were in great danger at every moment.

This is actually far from the truth. In fact, as Frank Furedi points out in his book *Paranoid Parenting* (see Chapter 8, Resources and Suggested Reading), we're safer in most ways than we've ever been. But because the press wants your custom, and because if you're worried you're more likely to buy newspapers and to tune into the television to stay informed, bad news is what you get.

Your tendency to worry will be even more entrenched if either of your parents was a worrier. You'll react like they did to most things unless you make a conscious decision not to do so. And sadly, there's plenty of material on offer out there to feed your worries, even though, in truth, that doomsday information is carefully selected.

3 Why try again? (once bitten twice shy)

If something frightens or hurts you, an understandable reaction is to avoid it from then on. However, thoughtless avoidance means that your opportunities to experience life, and to make the inevitable mistakes and to learn from them, will be reduced. Eventually you could become socially isolated or phobic, and, possibly, even depressed.

When you've been hurt or traumatised, it's better to stop and think about the aspects of that experience that were actually dangerous, and what you might do now other than simply avoiding the circumstances surrounding them. For example, if you're involved in a car crash, your first reaction may well be to avoid travelling in cars altogether. But this would restrict your life unduly. And if ever you had to drive, it would paradoxically leave you an inexperienced and therefore more dangerous driver than you were before the accident.

If, on the other hand, your reaction is to examine carefully the circumstances surrounding the car crash, you'll actually emerge from the experience as a safer driver and passenger. You might, for example, vow never again to accept a lift from anyone who's been drinking, or you might take lessons on how to drive more safely on motorways, or you might have your brakes checked more regularly. That way, not only would you continue to drive and therefore not be restricted, but you'd probably actually end up being a safer driver.

When you've been traumatised, your first reaction may be that it's best to avoid that activity altogether. However, it's better, as Susan Jeffers so famously said in her book (see Chapter 8, Resources and Suggested Reading) to 'feel the fear and do it anyway'.

4 But I really 'should'

Whenever you catch yourself saying that you 'should' do something, stop for a moment. What do you mean by that? If you mean that you want to do it, or that you feel that the effort you'll put in is worthwhile, you're quite likely to feel better if you act. If, however, you're driven by 'shoulds', that is, you're behaving out of a sense of obligation, there's a danger that you'll feel resentful. Your resistance will get in the way and make the task feel more like hard work than pleasure. This won't benefit you, and it's unlikely to benefit anyone else much either – what a waste of effort.

'Should' implies duty, or a reaction to someone else's demands, rather than a desire that springs from your own heart. Stop trying to please your mother, or your boss, or whoever it is, out of a sense of obligation. Put in effort when you yourself feel that there's a good reason for putting in that effort.

You'll probably find that this means you'll do many of the same things you did before. However, if you now do them because you've decided that they're worth doing, either for yourself or because you choose to please someone who matters to you, then the quality of what you do will change. You'll do a better job, you'll do things more cheerfully, you're more likely to persevere when the going gets tough and you'll feel more of a sense of achievement afterwards.

5 There's nothing I can do about it (learned helplessness)

Look out for comments like: 'What's the point?' or 'It's no use' to alert you to this mindset. 'Learned helplessness' is a

NEGATIVE THINKING | 103

wonderfully descriptive term coined by the American psychologist Martin Seligman. He noticed that many depressed people seem to expect to fail. When asked, these individuals told him that there wasn't much point in trying to improve their lives, because they were sure they'd fail. They no longer felt any connection between the effort they put in and the results they obtained.

Learned helplessness arises when you've been pushed into doing things without proper help or guidance, or when you're given too much responsibility too early in life, or sometimes simply because you've been unlucky too often. It can even arise because you've shown yourself to be competent; that is, if you're good at something, you're likely to be asked to do more of it. If you automatically take on more out of a sense of duty or because of a need to please others because of the 'shoulds', rather than because you've thought it through and you've decided that you want to rise to that particular challenge, then you may feel overloaded and start failing.

An important aspect of learned helplessness is selective remembering. If you've decided that there's no point in doing something, then you'll remember clearly when you fail and you're likely to overlook your successes. This mindset can be quite well entrenched, with roots that stretch far back into childhood. But as with most psychological problems, your chances of overcoming this mindset have more to do with how determined you are to change it than how long you've had the problem.

6 I'm afraid of failing

This limiting filter is characteristic of people with low or very fragile self-esteem. A fear of failure, of ridicule, or of rejection stops you from trying new things. That, in turn, limits your chances to become more competent, and so the chance of failing then becomes even more likely.

The people who harbour this fear assume that failure is a bad thing, and that it must be avoided at all costs. But failure is the best teacher you can have. When you succeed, you rarely consider how you acted. You simply bask in the praise you receive and in your own sense of achievement. It's only when you fail that you respond with a genuine will to learn. You're likely to ask yourself what went wrong and how you might improve so that you can succeed the next time. A favourite saying of mine (source unknown), is this: 'When you succeed, you party. When you fail, you learn something.'

7 It must be my fault

This attitude is found most often among first-born children. It can also arise in those who were given too much responsibility at too young an age. It's closely linked to the tyranny of the 'shoulds'.

If you're prone to over-responsibility, then whenever a task is in the offing you'll step forward, even if you don't want to do it. If you're prone to this personalisation, it means that whenever things go wrong, you'll immediately assume that you must be to blame. Individuals with these attitudes are likely to suffer from chronic exhaustion, and they rarely show any heartfelt enthusiasm. They have a strong sense of duty, but not much of a sense that life can be fun. They're often accused of having a victim mentality. Although their willingness to volunteer for duty may be appreciated, their sense of resignation about having to carry that load quickly makes them seem tiresome, and they often feel socially isolated.

8 I have to earn it; I don't deserve it

Of course, there are times when this mindset is totally appropriate. However, if it's applied indiscriminately it only leads to anxiety, and it also reinforces low self-esteem.

This attitude makes it impossible for you to accept gifts and compliments freely and gratefully. Rather than readily accepting what you're given, you start immediately to think about what you owe in return, or you start wondering whether you're worthy enough to receive the gift. If you're someone who thinks this way, events like Christmas may be come to be seen as a mountain of obligations, rather than as an opportunity to share time with people you love, and your life comes to resemble a balance sheet or a 'to-do' list.

9 I deserve it simply because I'm me

This is the flip side of the 'I don't deserve it' mentality. It's a relatively recent phenomenon and one that I hope will die young.

Overindulgent parents are to blame for inducing this belief in their children, and so are the unhelpful parenting 'experts' who insist that you should praise your child constantly, and for whatever he or she does.

When a child grows up demanding and receiving immediate gratification, such as when he or she's given the latest model of every toy or gadget available, when their lost and broken toys are replaced more or less at once and when they're told that however little effort or thought they put in it's wonderful, then it follows logically that they'll continue to expect this same treatment when they go out into the wider world. They won't find waiting easy, and they won't see the point of putting in effort themselves when they want something. They'll simply demand it and then expect it to appear.

This is a huge parenting mistake, and it represents the very worst side of consumerist culture (which we looked at in Chapter 1). It teaches irresponsibility, greed and selfishness. We in the wealthier parts of the world are, at last, waking up to our responsibility to save our planet, but this hasn't yet filtered down to some parental attitudes and practices.

In contrast, do you remember the sheer joy of buying something that you saved for weeks to afford? Do you remember your overwhelming pride when you brought home something to give your parents that you'd made yourself? What parent would wish to deny their child these pleasures?

Mercifully, because this is a relatively new attitude it isn't well established yet, and I'm hoping that it won't have a chance to become widespread. Any pleasure it gives a child is only fleeting, and if you adopt it, you'll only create children who'll become increasingly greedy and who'll never be wholly satisfied.

10 It's much worse than it seems (catastrophising)

Anyone who's highly anxious, particularly if he or she has been raised by anxious or pessimistic parents, is prone to adopting this mindset. Catastrophising can be defined as 'jumping from one result to overwhelming and dire or devastating consequences'. It encourages anxiety, and it can lead to panic attacks. You're particularly vulnerable to catastrophising over things that were hard earned and about things that mean a lot to you.

The media invite you to catastrophise because when it presents bad news it doesn't present a balanced picture. By concentrating on terrible events but not saying how rarely they occur, the media in fact often give the impression that they are commonplace.

It's much better to think about what you can do to help when something terrible happens (for example, give a donation to a relevant appeal fund) rather than to jump to the conclusion that it may soon happen to you.

11 It's one or the other (black-and-white thinking)

Anxiety polarises thought. When you're stressed and anxious, particularly when you live in this state chronically, your conclusions will often be couched in terms of 'either/or', 'one way or the other' or 'all or nothing'. This reflects the brain's need to simplify everything when it senses danger. In dangerous situations there's no time for lengthy debates or thoughtful discussions. Threats to your safety demand an immediate reaction. You ask yourself: 'Can I escape or do I have to stay and fight? I must decide – now!'

However, as we've learned, the threats that maintain anxiety are *potential* threats rather than real ones. Time is needed to verify how likely the threat actually is. You need to think carefully to come up with a number of solutions so that the best ones may be chosen. There's not much to be gained by running from 'potentials' or fighting 'maybes'.

12 It's bound to rain (Eyeore thinking)

If you have this mindset, your thoughts and your reasoning aren't usually wrong, they're just not helpful. Say, for example, that the sun is shining, you have a day off work and you've planned a day at the beach. If you're a maladaptive thinker, the first thing you'll do is to check the long-term weather forecast. If there's any chance of rain – any chance at all – you'll either cancel your trip to the beach or you'll spend most of your time checking for signs of impending rain. Maladaptive thinkers, like Eyeore (in *Winnie the Pooh*), always dwell on the worst possibilities, and in so doing they often miss the good moments.

These, then, are the negative beliefs that I've come across most often in my clinics. They go hand in hand with low self-esteem and feelings of unworthiness, and they only encourage anxiety, pessimism and discontent – they're never helpful.

If you've now realised that you're carrying any of these negative beliefs around with you, I'm sure you'd like to get rid of them. Cognitive-behaviour therapy is currently the most popular way to help you do this. It's a practical, structured method that helps you to identify your negative beliefs, test them out and challenge them through debate and experimentation, and then to discard them. If this approach appeals to you, I suggest you seek out a good cognitive-behaviour therapist, and/or refer to the relevant books I've listed in Chapter 8, Resources and Suggested Reading.

Such a structured approach doesn't, however, appeal to everyone. Nor is everyone comfortable focusing primarily on what's wrong with their belief system. If you're one of these people, you might prefer instead simply to start practising positive ways of thinking right away.

A more positive mindset

When I work with patients, I prefer to build on their positive beliefs and attitudes rather than to attack the negative ones. My aim is to help them bring their positive beliefs to the forefront of their minds and to start thinking about these beliefs so that there are no longer any opportunities for negative thinking. This is also easier than fighting negative beliefs, because positive thinking is so rewarding. You'll start to feel much better about your life, and to look forward to your future once you accept and focus on the positive beliefs.

During every session of therapy, my patients and I look out for their positive statements. Whenever they make a statement that reinforces an existing positive belief or starts to build a new one, we condense that statement into a single statement or phrase. For homework, patients then make copies of that statement and put it where they'll see it most often:

on their refrigerators, on their computer screens, in the front of their diaries. These constant reminders work their way into everyday thinking and positive challenges start to replace negative, destructive beliefs.

Sound too easy to be effective? All I can say is that it's worked brilliantly for my patients. And because this approach has no harmful side effects of which I'm aware, you can't really lose by trying it out.

I've developed what I call 'challenges' as part of this process. You'll notice that some of them challenge a specific negative belief, while others challenge several of the negative beliefs simultaneously. Don't worry too much about which negative belief each of the challenges replaces, because I don't want you to think like that. I don't want you, in fact, to think about the negative beliefs at all.

The challenges

Simply read through all of the challenges, and then choose whichever appeal to you. Make several copies of each of the ones you've chosen, and put those copies where you'll see them most often. Then you, too, will know what positive thinking can do to empower you.

1 There are always more than two possibilities and I'm going to look for them

Thinking in absolutes, that is, as if there are only two possible solutions to any dilemma, is very limiting. It's like viewing the world only in black and white, rather than appreciating the many colours and shades in the world.

A good way to break this habit is to play the 'And what else?' game. At the end of each day, write down two occasions when you felt disappointed or upset. Ask yourself what made you feel this way and write down your answer. Then ask yourself 'OK, that's a possibility. But what else might have made me feel this way?' Keep asking this question until you simply can't come up with another possibility. This technique is also known as brainstorming.

Be as fanciful as you like; in fact, the wilder your speculations, the more you'll stimulate and widen your mind to further possibilities and the more creative you'll become.

2 I can choose where I focus my attention

Because you're constantly bombarded with stimuli (as I described in 'Information overload' in Chapter 1), it's not possible to pay equal attention to everything. You'll constantly be choosing what to attend to and what to ignore.

If you remain aware of this freedom and make good use of it, it can create an upward spiral. When you choose to focus on the positive aspects in your life, you're likely to feel better. If you're feeling better, you'll be more likely to notice the good things around you. For this alone, it's worth giving your attention to the positive aspects of your life.

There are many other rewards of choosing the positive as well. Research has shown that happy people, that is, people with a positive outlook on life tend to live longer, have a better chance of recovering from illness and trauma and are also considered more attractive by others.

In general, if you expect to do well, it's more likely that you will. If you expect to find that what's around you is pleasant and enjoyable, it's more likely to be so. In simple terms, you usually get what you expect.

A good way to start changing your outlook is to keep a positive-events diary. At the end of each day, write down the three happiest or most rewarding events of that day, however small they seem. It's good to do this just before bedtime; that way, you'll end your day with a positive outlook.

After two weeks, in addition to writing down those three

events, write down one positive moment that you plan to have the next day. This means that you'll now be focusing not only on the recent past, but also on the near future.

Then, one week later, add one further entry each evening. Write down one thing that you can appreciate, right at that moment.

Continue keeping this record until it becomes a habit.

3 If I calm down first it will be easier to solve my problems

Logic and anxiety don't coexist happily. If you're generally stressed it will be a great deal more difficult for you to become an effective problem solver. It's therefore extremely important that you remember to set aside some time every day to be calm and to practise focusing on something positive. This will help you to increase your ability to concentrate. Make a habit of starting and ending each day with 40 paced breaths, or spend ten minutes each day practising mindfulness, yoga or any other focusing exercise. Finish the exercise by bringing to mind an enjoyable experience.

4 'Should' doesn't mean I have to do it

When you say you 'should' do something, you're very likely to be talking about an obligation to an imposed set of beliefs, or a need to please someone other than yourself. You'll rarely do anything you 'should' do with joy and enthusiasm. If on the other hand, you'd 'love' to do something, or you 'want' to do it, you'll almost certainly enjoy that experience. It will feel much more like your own choice, and the experience will contribute to your sense of well-being generally.

There will of course be occasions when a 'should' is unavoidable. For example, if you have a dog, you really should feed and exercise it even when you don't feel very much like doing so, because your dog is entirely dependent on you for its very existence. But even here there's latitude: if you were to say, 'I really should feed the dog,' you won't enjoy doing so. But if instead you were to say to yourself 'It's a bother sometimes to feed my dog, but she's so grateful when I do feed her that it always makes me glad,' then the task of feeding her will feel like a more worthwhile decision.

The best way, therefore, to deal with the 'shoulds' in your life is to start by asking yourself what ideals or what person you're trying to please. Is the appeasement really necessary? If not, free yourself from that obligation. If so, reword what you say to yourself about that task so that it becomes less of an obligation and more of a desire.

5 I can take responsibility but I don't need to take on guilt

Guilt is a wasteful emotion. Why spend your time feeling bad about something that's already happened? It will be something that you can't go back in time and change anyway.

When things have gone wrong and mistakes have been made, it's important to accept your rightful share of responsibility. But nothing is gained by punishing yourself for it. It's better to think about what you can do to improve things now, and to ensure that the outcome is a better one the next time a similar situation arises.

The next time you catch yourself feeling guilty, ask yourself instead what you can do to improve the situation in the future.

6 Never mind the prizes, I'll praise myself for my effort

If you want to maximise the chance of feeling pleased with yourself, focus on the effort you expend rather than on the prizes you're awarded. It's important to remember that the outcome depends not only on your own efforts but also on who makes the judgements, what conditions you face and who competes against you. Many factors that determine an outcome are not, therefore, under your control. Learn to praise yourself for what you can guarantee – your effort – rather than for the outcome of that effort.

7 My best yardstick for measuring progress is to compare myself with myself

A common negative thought is that you're not as good as someone else. For every one of you this will be true regarding at least one skill or ability that you have. Rather than feeling defeated by this fact, it's best not to spend a great deal of time dwelling on it.

A much more sensible approach to improving your skills and abilities is to compare your present performance with your previous performances. If you're doing as well or better than you've done before, you can congratulate yourself. If you don't perform as well, you'll need to find ways to improve, safe in the knowledge that you know you can do better because you've done so before.

Of course, there's a place for comparing your performance to that of others. We all face competition in everyday life – for jobs, in exams and for promotions. But if you can accept that some people will always be better than you are at some things, then losing need no longer trigger negative thoughts. You can simply conclude that, on those occasions, you weren't the best qualified for that job, or best prepared to win that race or whatever. But, as long as you improve with regard to yourself you have good reason to be proud of your performance. And, if you don't improve, you have an opportunity to learn something.

This way of thinking carries a bonus. When you stop needing to outperform others in order to feel good about yourself, other people will seem less threatening, and the chance of developing negative attitudes about them decreases. The world about you will start to seem a much happier place. You can even feel pleased for others when they win, and this will cause others to like you more.

8 Imagery will help me to think positively

When you imagine life as you'd like it to be, particularly if you do so while you're fully relaxed, your mind accepts that ideal as if it already exists – or at the very least as if it could be highly likely.

Imagery provides clear direction, and, in order to imagine your life as you wish it to be, you need to be sure of exactly what you wish. This sounds obvious, but so often in our lives we don't stop long enough really to define our aims. No wonder many of us feel chronically dissatisfied. If you don't know what the destination looks like, how can you know when you've arrived?

Furthermore, you're more likely to feel energised and positive if you fill your mind with what you do want, rather than if you simply try to get rid of the negative messages you don't want. The rationale for this is the same as it is for using thought blockers to alleviate anxiety (see Chapter 3). Trying to get rid of what you don't want means you're paying attention to what you don't want. What you're doing, in effect, is giving the negative thoughts power as well as pride of place in your mind. Instead, it's much more effective to fill your mind with what you do want, leaving no opportunity for any negative thoughts.

It's important to plan ahead when you want to use positive imagery. Because this is such a powerful technique, you'll want to be sure that you're well prepared and that you're in the most receptive state possible, so that what you visualise will definitely help you. Follow these steps:

1 Start by learning how to put yourself into a highly receptive state by using the graded relaxation exercise described in Chapter 3. Practise until you feel you are able to relax fully and completely.

2 Next, choose a negative belief that you'd like to eliminate. Perhaps you're convinced that no one would want to get to know you, or that no one would be interested in you. Choose a specific situation, preferably something that will actually happen soon, such as a party you've been invited to attend or an office outing you've agreed to go on. (Notice that we're being very specific. Even though this particular occasion doesn't address all of the negative feelings you might have about yourself, it's necessary to start with something specific, as imagery works on specifics. Once you've imagined and challenged just one example that supports your negative belief, the entire belief weakens. Two or three examples are usually enough to break its power completely.)

3 You're now ready to use the imagery technique. Find somewhere quiet and comfortable. Turn off your phones and ask not to be disturbed for about ten to 20 minutes. Start by doing 40 paced breaths and take yourself into deep relaxation. Once you're fully relaxed, imagine going into that party. Imagine yourself well dressed, smiling and calm, and looking around the room in anticipation of meeting someone interesting.

4 You now notice someone looking your way. Imagine returning his or her glance. Smile, and see the stranger approach you. Ask a friendly question (you'll need to think about this before you relax, so you can imagine something specific). Look at him or her as they begin to tell you about how they know the host, or why they've come to the party tonight. You needn't have created the entire conversation, only a good opening line or two. What you need to do after the initial greeting is to hold the image of the two of you talking together happily. It's important that you imagine yourself showing a genuine interest in whoever you're talking to, because a person is judged to be most attractive to another person when there's a show of genuine interest.

5 You can now use a fade-out technique: 'freeze-frame' the image of the two of you talking easily and comfortably with one another, and move back from it mentally, as if you're watching a film where the scene is fading in preparation for another, later scene.

6 Now let the next scene take shape: imagine that it's some time later and you're still at the party and you see yourself chatting in a small group, perhaps three or four of you. You're laughing and talking and you're all enjoying yourselves generally. Then someone looks at their watch and says they must leave. First, however, he or she turns to you and says that he'd like to meet up again and could they have your contact details. You then imagine all four of you exchanging details, giving each other warm hugs or handshakes and leaving the party. Finally, imagine yourself on the journey home, smiling happily as you think about the delightful evening.

7 Plan to practise your particular scene at least three, and better yet, five times, before it actually takes place, or before you try it out in your daily life. And finally, just before you enter into the real-life situation, do some paced breathing.

I've given you this example in such detail so that you can see just how specific you need to be if the imagery technique is to be effective for you. It must be realistic, and preferably it should represent an opportunity that will actually take place soon. You need to be as detailed and as accurate as you can be. In the process, you'll no doubt learn a great deal that will come in handy when the actual event takes place. In our example, you'd have to think of some specific ways to introduce yourself to a stranger. In doing so, you'll remind yourself about the importance of showing a genuine interest in others, about the need to ask questions, and about the importance of listening carefully.

The imagery technique can systematically replace your negative beliefs with more positive and adaptive ideas. Furthermore, it entails learning skills that you'll find helpful in real-life situations. This technique is also enjoyable, because it allows you to use your imagination and to think positively about your future.

It's important to remember that you weren't born with the negative beliefs you hold now. You learned them, every one of them, and their only validity is your belief in them. Why continue to reinforce something that makes you unhappy and that stops you doing what you want to do?

Remember, too, that imagery can always help you to improve on your situation. If things go well, you're another step on the way to disproving a negative belief. If things don't turn out as you had hoped, you can go over the situation mentally and freeze-frame your image at the point where things started to go wrong. Then you can reconstruct the scene in your mind and, this time, you can make sure that things turn out well. Then you'll also be able to tell yourself what you need to do differently next time.

This systematic practice of increasing and enhancing your skills will further weaken any negative beliefs you may still hold about what you can learn and what you can do.

9 I believe in myself (mirror talk)

We pay attention to the sound of our own voice. You can use this fact to great advantage when you're learning to think positively. A number of motivational writers such as Claude Bristol, and cognitive-behaviour psychologists such as Albert Ellis (see Chapter 8, Resources and Suggested Reading for their books), encourage the use of self-talk – or more specifically here, mirror talk.

Try this the next time you want to convince yourself – or anyone else for that matter – of your worth. The idea of practising speeches this way isn't new: it's said that Winston Churchill is only one of a number of famous orators who practised their speeches in front of a mirror before delivering them to others. You can use this to boost your eloquence in job interviews, to help you get a place at university, to increase the chances that you'll convince someone to back you for a business enterprise or simply to bolster your own self-esteem generally.

About a week before the actual event start to organise yourself: write out, word for word, what you'd hope to say if you had all the time in the world to say it, and if you were feeling totally calm. If you can, imagine any objections others might raise and write out your answers to these as well. Next, condense your 'speech' on to one A4-size piece of paper. Now you're ready to start practising.

Each day, for at least three days, stand in front of a large mirror and look directly at yourself. State clearly exactly what you want to say when the actual moment arrives. If you need to do so, keep notes at your side and glance at them as necessary. If you don't know for sure what you'll be asked in the actual interview or whatever it is, then you can use your mirror time instead for a mirror talk:

Stand in front of the mirror and say something like this: 'I'm going to do a fantastic job in this interview. I'll speak clearly, and I'll answer all the questions confidently. I know I'll do my best.' Or try this: 'I know I'll be able to convince X that this is a great idea. I know it is, and I really want to share it with everyone.'

You'll definitely feel ridiculous at first, everyone does. It's fine to laugh, in fact, laughter is an excellent release of tension. But then get down to serious practice, because it really will pay off. And all the time you're practising something this positive, your mind will be filled with positive inspirations, crowding out any negative thoughts.

In summary, then, when you use mirror talk, use these guidelines:

- Write out what you're going to say, word for word, before you start practising in front of the mirror. That way, you'll appear authoritative and self-assured.

- Look directly at yourself when you speak. Direct eye contact encourages you to pay full attention to what you're saying.

- Always phrase your statements positively. For example, say: 'I'm going to speak clearly,' rather than: 'I mustn't stutter.'

- Be as specific as possible. For example, it's much more powerful to say: 'I'm going to complete the top two jobs on my list today,' than it is to say: 'I'm going to work hard.'

Enjoy this technique. It's an opportunity to put yourself in the best possible light, and it's also amusing.

10 What would I say to my best friend about this?

It's interesting to note that most of us are judgemental and harsh with regard to ourselves, and yet we're kind and generous when it comes to our friends. If you're hurt or make a mistake, you may well wonder how you could have been so clumsy. If a friend makes a mistake, you're quite likely to forgive him or her, and if they've been hurt, you'll offer comfort. Why the double standard? It won't help you, encourage you or motivate you, to be so harsh with yourself.

The next time something goes badly for you, or the next time you make a mistake, stop yourself as soon as you become aware of your self-criticism. Instead, ask yourself how you would react if this had happened to your best friend. What explanations would you offer? What questions would you ask that would help him or her to feel better, or that would allow them to learn something from what happened? Take this same approach with regard to yourself.

11 I won't be afraid to ask for help when I need it

It's difficult to know where to draw the line between trying to overcome your fears and anxieties on your own, and obtaining the help of a professional. Of course, it's always nice to have professional help, or at least advice, because it's quicker and because it feels safer to let an expert tell you what to do.

However, professional help can be expensive, and/or you may have to wait a long time to get the help you need. And, in truth, although it may be surer and quicker to be told the best way to go about solving a problem, you won't feel as satisfied as when you figure it out for yourself.

That said, there are situations in which it's wiser to seek help. If your worries or fears are so intrusive that they prevent you from going about your normal daily life, or if, at times, you feel so low that you don't think life is worth living, or if you're suffering from clinical depression (if you're not sure, see your GP), then I strongly recommend that you seek professional help. Talk to your GP, as he or she can help you to decide the approach that's best for you.

CASE STUDY: **Martin**

When he was 50, Martin was referred to me by the psychiatrist who had helped him overcome a serious depression. He was living on his own, and had worked as an IT consultant for the last 15 years, having previously worked as an electrical engineer.

Martin was an only child. His parents had been told that they couldn't have children, so his mother was astonished and delighted to find that she was pregnant with Martin when she was 42. He grew up, much loved, in a fairly remote village where he had attended the local village school. He told me that there weren't many children in the school, but among them were two friends with whom he still socialised occasionally. He'd gone on to study engineering and business at university.

Martin told me he'd always enjoyed his work. He also enjoyed good food and wine and, before becoming depressed, he'd socialised regularly with colleagues, organising outings to various pubs and restaurants, although he said that he often felt that, because he was single, he was the odd one out. He'd never married and had never had a serious relationship.

His father had died when he was 20, and he'd spent much of his free time over the last 28 years looking after his increasingly frail mother. He often had to cancel his own plans at the last minute if his mother needed him. He had nursed her through her final illness, and he was at her bedside when she died.

It was just after her death two years previously that Martin had become severely depressed. During his depression, he became convinced that life had passed him by, and that he was now too old to be considered attractive as a potential partner. He assumed as well that most people already had partners. His GP referred him to the local consultant psychiatrist, who put him on a course of anti-depressants and had supported him as he gradually returned to work. Once he had resumed work, she suggested that he might like to have some cognitive-behaviour therapy to deal with his negative beliefs.

Now that he was back at work and his antidepressant medication had stabilised his mood, Martin was sleeping better and feeling a bit better in himself. However, when I first met him he told me that he was convinced that 'there is nothing to look forward to, because I'm too old to start a life now'. He said that he wasn't sure what it would mean to 'have a life', although he wanted a more active social life, and he wanted to be slimmer and fitter. He told me that he felt he was too old and too fat to appeal to any woman, although he very much wanted to meet a partner.

He agreed, rather reluctantly, to begin by examining how valid his belief was that it was too late to start a social life. He told me that all his friends already had partners and families, and that he was the only one on his own. He also told me that the people he knew didn't really want a loner included in their lives. As a home-work assignment, he agreed to write out a list of his colleagues and friends, and to describe their partners. He also agreed to compile a list of his most recent social outings, when they had taken place and who accom-panied him.

When Martin came to see me next, he told me he'd been surprised to find that of the 12 people in his office, two were divorced and one was, like him, single. He had also forgotten that one of his two old school friends was divorced. He remembered that although he'd not been out socially since his mother died, he'd begun to recall how much he'd enjoyed outings with friends regularly before her death, and also that they'd often told him what a good organiser he was. He was now less reluctant to agree to approach some of his friends with the aim of going out to a restaurant one night soon.

He returned three weeks later in a much more positive frame of mind. He had asked two of his friends whether they would like to go out to a restaurant, and they had been happy to agree. In fact, he said another colleague overheard him discussing this idea and asked if he could join them as well. This pleased him enormously. He'd enjoyed the evening out, and he and his friends had already arranged another outing.

Martin was, however, much more reluctant to believe that he would ever meet anyone new who would enjoy his company, particularly any women. He told me that because he was 'old and fat', he felt sure that he would be rejected. For his next homework assignment, he agreed to find out just how overweight he actually was, and what could be done about it. He agreed to make an appointment with his GP for a check-up.

The next time we met, Martin told me what he'd learned. His GP said he needed to lose 6kg (1 stone) and to take more aerobic exercise. He didn't feel he had the willpower to lose the weight on his own, so he decided to join the local Weight Watchers group. He'd been with them in the past and he told me that they'd helped him reach his goals quickly. Another benefit of joining a new group, Martin commented, might be that he'd meet some new people.

We had now met five times, and Martin was feeling a great deal more optimistic. He had dispensed with believing that everyone else has a family life and that he couldn't enjoy himself unless he had a partner, and he was beginning to think much more about how to enjoy himself. He was no longer convinced that he needed a partner to be considered acceptable.

However, it was when he was alone at night that Martin still found it hard to ignore his belief, which he clung to quite strongly, that he was unattractive. We concluded that it might be better to fill the time with other thoughts, rather than to challenge his negative self-image directly.

Martin had long been interested in meditation, and he had heard that there were classes in a nearby village, so he decided to enrol once the new term started. He found that practising meditation calmed him greatly. It also prevented the negative thoughts from taking hold at night, which was the time when he was feeling at his most lonely and vulnerable.

At our next session, we talked about Martin's conviction that he needed to be slim before anyone would be interested in him. I described an experiment where men judged a woman to be beautiful simply because she showed an interest in them, and he was intrigued. We then rehearsed the sorts of questions he might ask someone he had just met that would encourage her to talk about herself. He was sceptical, but agreed to try this at Weight Watchers.

Martin came to his next session full of enthusiasm. He told me that he had approached a woman he'd been admiring at Weight Watchers and asked her some questions that got her talking about herself. In the end, they had stayed on for nearly an hour after the meeting and she asked if they could meet for a coffee again soon. He was delighted, and said he was now prepared to admit that perhaps a genuine interest in others was at least as important as good looks when it came to meeting people.

How this applies to you

As you can see from the progress Martin made, it can sometimes be tricky to decide on the best way to adopt a more positive mindset. The easiest and most effective way, as I've said, is simply to adopt more positive ways of thinking; that is, by focusing on the challenges rather than clinging to any self-defeating views you may hold.

However, there will be times when your well-established negative beliefs may stand in direct contradiction to one or more of the challenges. Whenever that's true, you'll have to think of ways to test your negative beliefs. In Martin's case, for example, actually counting the number of single people among his friends was a real eye opener. He saw that although he was in the minority, he was certainly not alone. Looking at things in a fresh light helped him remember, too, that he had often been complimented on his ability to organise social events. He realised that his status as a single person actually had a positive side: he was someone who had the time and opportunities to make arrangements for his friends to meet up.

If you need to check out the truth of any of your beliefs, the best way to decide how to do so is to use a variant of the Friend Test. That is, ask yourself what you'd suggest to a friend of yours if he or she held a belief that only caused them misery. Then once you have the facts, you'll either want to forget about the belief or reword it so that it's more accurate, and, crucially, more likely to encourage you to think about and do some of the things you really enjoy.

6

Loss of Contentment

For in the dew of little things the heart finds its morning and is refreshed.

The Prophet
Kahlil Gibran

On the face of it, Simon had everything. The elder of two boys, he'd been on the sports team and played in the jazz band at school. His A level results had been good and he was accepted by his first choice of university where he'd read law and enjoyed a good social life. After university, he'd had no trouble finding a job, and, at 29, was made a partner in his firm of solicitors – the youngest person to be offered this position. He'd had a number of girlfriends, although none of them serious, and he went out drinking with colleagues or friends from his sports club at least once a week. And yet, shortly after his thirtieth birthday, he'd plunged into a serious depression. Why?

'I just thought, well, here I am. I've done it all, everything I set out to achieve. And now I just keep thinking, is that it? Is that all there is to it? What was the point of all that?'

Unfortunately, Simon's not alone. As I described in Chapter 1, in 'Confusing wanting with needing', because of the constant pressure from advertisements, we've lost sight of the difference between what we actually need and what we want. A recent survey showed that we're feeling less happy now than ever before, and that this is particularly true for those in the 30 to 40 year age group. Materially, it would seem that we have it all, but, apparently, it doesn't feel like that. Why not? Is our modern focus on self-promotion, acquisition and goal attainment not that wonderful? No, I don't think it is, not at all.

The stories of unhappiness and emptiness that I hear in my clinic, from individuals with so much promise, tell me that something has gone very, very wrong. It seems to me that there are a number of myths that we hold account for the all too prevalent sense of hopelessness and loneliness. I'm going to describe each of them, and then I'll suggest an amendment that could lead to a much better chance of finding contentment.

If you like, you can simply write each of the amendments on slips of paper and place these strategically around your home. You might also download them on to your computers and mobiles. That way, you'll be reminded of them regularly. This is the same approach we used in Chapter 5 (with the challenges) to help you discard your negative beliefs. However, if you prefer a more structured approach, you may wish to try some of the practical suggestions that I've included in each section. These are just a sample of the many possibilities, but hopefully they'll stimulate ideas of your own. The aim of the suggestions is to help you to live in a way that's more in tune with the amendments – a more positive and satisfying way of living.

The seven modern myths

Here, then, are the seven modern myths as I see them, together with their more constructive, more empowering amendments:

Myth1: My life should make sense

Many of us love to relax with a good novel, but not so many of us consider biographies as entertaining. Why is this? The reason, as most writers will readily admit, is that it's easier to create characters whose lives make sense than it does to make sense out of real characters' lives, and this comes through in the writing.

The reason that we love novels so much is that a large part of our brain is dedicated to making sense of things. This is a survival mechanism characteristic of all higher primates; it's what allows us to adapt when circumstances change, and to survive when unexpected and terrible things happen. Our need to understand is a strong one, and often we don't feel safe until what's happening makes sense to us.

However, when it comes to living your daily life and predicting what's going to happen, there's a trade-off. The more predictable your life is, the more boring, restricted and rigid it can become. There's little room for excitement, discovery or creativity in a totally predictable life.

Only when most of the pieces of the puzzle are in place, that is, near the end of your life, will there be any real chance of making sense of it. That's why the need to reminisce grows ever stronger as we grow older. It's at this time that the chances of making sense of our lives increase. Most of us want to feel reassured that our lives followed a meaningful pattern and that there was a reason for our existence.

So, although you can see the reason why this myth is so powerful, I hope you won't try to make it a major feature in your life. If you do, you'll lose so many chances for excitement and challenge. Therefore, let's amend the first myth.

My life doesn't have to make sense right now

SUGGESTIONS

Focus on the small things

Set yourself the target of achieving one accomplishment each day, something small enough that you can be sure to complete it. It's best if this is either something where you can see the result easily (for example, repotting a house plant or sewing a button back on a shirt), or one that pleases another person (phone a friend, or remember someone's birthday by sending a card). Small tasks are satisfying, and because you can complete them, it feels as if you're going somewhere. And the small things have a way of interconnecting to become larger things, and to introduce you to new ideas and directions.

Rediscover early interests

What did you enjoy doing when you were a child? How did you spend your day? To recall some of your early enthusiasms and to reignite some of them will not only be enjoyable but also give you a sense of continuity. If you can't remember what you once enjoyed doing, ask family members or look through old diaries, photo albums or school reports.

Keep a diary

Write down what happens in your life, even if you only do so from time to time. When you read back over your record, in retrospect you'll see meaning that wasn't apparent at the time. You'll also retain many memories that might otherwise disappear from your awareness.

Myth 2: I must be afraid, I must be very afraid

This myth is primarily reinforced through the media. Most of what we hear on the news and read in the press is bad news. As I've already said repeatedly, this is because bad news sells better than good news, and the media is in the business of making a profit rather than of offering you an unbiased and balanced picture of the world. Bad news suggests that we're in some sort of danger, so our natural response is to want to understand, to know more about these threats to our well-being. We believe that if we can stay informed, we'll then have the best chance of protecting ourselves and our loved ones from whatever danger is currently being discussed. So, bad news makes us feel discontented and anxious – and keen to buy more information.

There's nothing wrong with keeping yourself informed about what's going on in the world. However, in order to obtain a balanced picture you'll need to limit your intake of news, and seek out other sources of information, in particular your own direct experience.

We'll amend the second myth now:

I'll approach each day with a healthy curiosity

SUGGESTIONS

Look further than the headlines
Spend as much time each day absorbing educational or entertaining information as you spend absorbing the (bad) news. It's not difficult to find this kind of information: look at the features sections in newspapers and choose magazine articles that will educate or uplift. Don't simply turn on the television to see what's on; instead choose the programmes you want to watch the night before, with a balanced view in mind.

Choose carefully when to listen to the (bad) news
If you find it difficult to get going in the morning, a head

full of bad news and disasters won't help. If you wish to be aware of current events, you might prefer to do so at lunchtime or in the early evening, when you're more able to listen objectively. If, on the other hand, nothing dampens your spirits in the morning but you often feel tired and overwhelmed in the evening, listen to the news in the morning so you can stay up to date with current events.

Notice what's happening now

In your own world, pay attention to what's going on around you. It may seem unnecessary to remember to do this, but so many people go through their days unaware of their immediate surroundings. Make it a practice to notice at least one thing that pleases you each day: whether the shops had the sort of fresh fruit you particularly enjoy, or your son or daughter had a good day at school and wanted to tell you about it, or the computer never crashed. It's all too easy to forget that much of what happens in your immediate surroundings is pleasant, or, at least, not negative.

Focus regularly on a feeling of peace

You probably guessed that I would suggest this, but daily 'centring' time – 40 paced breaths , or ten minutes of yoga, or mindfulness – will help you to maintain a sense of calm that will then keep you steady if you do hear unpleasant news.

Myth 3: If someone doesn't like me exactly as I am, it's best to dump him or her and find someone who does

This kind of attitude towards personal relationships goes hand in hand with our consumer economy. The idea in both cases is that if something doesn't work, it's not your responsibility and you needn't bother to fix it – just throw it away. In terms of our planet, we're waking up at last to the fact that this attitude could destroy the whole of our physical environment. Such an attitude, when applied to relationships, can also destroy the whole of our psychological well-being.

Furthermore, you'll feel the greatest pride in the things you work hard to attain. Things that come easily may still be enjoyed of course, but your enjoyment will be so much more profound, and will last much longer if you put effort into attaining them yourself.

If you're never challenged; if you never work through difficulties, you're unlikely to experience real satisfaction. Furthermore, if you walk out whenever things go wrong, you'll never learn much. You're most likely to walk into another situation and repeat the same mistakes that you made before.

In the longer term, intimate relationships are bound to encounter difficulties, and they require constant input and effort if they are to last. I still remember something one of my patients said when he found out that his wife was having an affair. 'Over the years, my good friends kept telling me how hard it was for them to make their marriages work, and what time and effort it was costing them. I always used to laugh at them. "Mine's a breeze," I'd say, "Just pretend you're listening and don't argue. It's just so much easier." I wish now that I'd really listened to her. I wish so much I'd tried harder to make things work.'

This is not to say that all relationships must necessarily continue. There are times when you have to admit that it just isn't in the best interests of either of you to continue. This applies to friendships, marriages and business partnerships alike. But even in those cases, the effort you put in to try to make things work will have been worthwhile. You'll find that in the longer term, it will be far easier to accept that a relationship had to end if you know that you tried your best to make it work.

There's one other point that I think is important: not

everyone needs intimacy to feel content. Individuals differ enormously in their need for intimacy, and one part of discovering yourself is to learn how much intimacy is right for you. But we all need some degree of connectedness to other human beings, and whatever your optimal level of intimacy or connectedness is to others, you'll be more content if you put time and effort into maintaining and valuing it.

Therefore, let's reword the third myth:

No man is an island. It will be well worth my while to put care and effort into my relationships

SUGGESTIONS

Show that you care

Familiarity doesn't necessarily breed contempt, but it does seem to breed indifference. Try to do something every day, however small, that shows you care about the people who matter to you. Offer a sincere compliment, a genuine question about their well-being, or a small gesture that you know they'll appreciate. Each will probably take less than a minute, but will mean so much.

Communicate clearly

So many opportunities to communicate are missed every day. Good communication is the foundation of a stable relationship, yet all too often we don't take the time to keep those channels open. Turn off the television during mealtimes, and try to have one meal together every day with everybody in your household. Ask questions and really listen to the answers, while looking directly at the person you're talking to. You needn't have deep, soul-searching sessions every day, but keeping the channels of communication open by showing genuine interest in those who matter most to you will always be worth the effort.

Remember what counts to others

If you're really listening to those around you, you'll know what matters most to them and you can honour that. Simple things, such as respecting the fact that you love to chatter in the morning but your partner prefers to read the paper; remembering that your teenager likes tea rather than coffee at breakfast, or remembering to phone or send a card on a friend's birthday shows that you're thinking about the other person. These are only small gestures, I know. But the small things are often those most fondly remembered, and are the ones that can bolster a relationship that's become dull or mundane.

Make a regular date together

When I work with couples whose relationships are in trouble, one of the things we try to do is re-establish the 'date'. Once a week or fortnight, the couple arranges to spend an evening together without the distractions of television or children. Although often uncomfortable at first, most couples tell me that this special time becomes very enjoyable. This applies equally well with children, particularly if you have more than one. When my children were young, once a fortnight I took each one out for tea after school. The child feels valued, and there's a chance for some real conversations.

Myth 4: I must look busy, and I must always permit interruptions

When I was a child, I found an advertisement in the Lost and Found section of our local newspaper that I've never forgotten. I don't know who put it there, or why, but even as a child it struck me as important. Here's the ad:

'LOST: Yesterday, somewhere between sunrise and sunset, two golden hours, each set with sixty diamond minutes. No reward is offered, for they are gone forever.'

Trite, I know, but also true. Once the present moment is gone you'll never get it back again, not ever. Yet how often do you actually live in your irreplaceable present moments? How often do you turn off your phones, your iPods and your computers and just look about you?

At the beginning of her therapy, I set what seemed a simple task for one of my patients, an accountant in a busy high-street firm. I asked her to spend two minutes each day doing nothing. For the first ten days, she couldn't do it; she simply couldn't stop herself wondering who might be calling or what she could be planning. It took her more than a week to teach herself to devote just 1 per cent of her entire day to being wholly in the present moment.

There's the most wonderful scene in the film *Hook* that illustrates this point well. In this film, Peter Pan, played by Robin Williams, is now a successful lawyer with a young family of his own. He keeps promising to attend his children's school plays or sports events – the things that matter so much to them – but he always has some more important interruption at work, and he misses all their big events. But, there is a moment, at home, when his children try to get him to play with them. However, his mobile rings yet again, and he shouts at them to go away and be quiet so he can answer it. His wife is no longer able to contain herself and she tries to talk to him about what he's doing. His mobile rings again and this time he interrupts her to answer it. At this point, in exasperation, she throws the mobile out of the window and tells him that he's losing the precious, irretrievable opportunities to be with his children now, while they're young. 'You must be careful, Peter,' she warns him, 'because you're missing IT.' And he was – he'd forgotten how to live for now.

Think about how much impatience and distress you cause yourself by constantly allowing interruptions (as we saw in Chapter 1). If you're always alert for and expecting distractions, if you're always poised for the phone or a text message to interrupt you, then you'll always be in a state of tension, and you'll never be able to experience the joy of losing yourself fully in the moment, of appreciating completely what you're doing.

Another way to shatter contentment is to decide that you're waiting. Something may be about to happen that you wish to do: perhaps you're in a queue to buy a ticket for the cinema. But it's up to you whether you consider that you're 'waiting' during that time in the queue, or whether you're people-watching, or reading about all the films on offer, or whatever. If you choose to wait, you're relegating that time in the queue to the dustbin. You're telling yourself that now is not where you want to be. How unpleasant and unsatisfying that time will then be! Why choose to consider that time a wait, when instead you could enjoy those moments? Either way, you'll still get to see the film.

Let's now amend the fourth myth:

I'll try to live fully in the moment as often as I can

SUGGESTIONS

Do nothing

Set aside two minutes a day in which you do nothing. Sit somewhere comfortable, turn off your phones and anything else that might intrude and simply sit there. You can close your eyes if you wish; if you don't, just let your eyes rest on your surroundings, but try not to process or think about what you see. If you start thinking about anything; for example, making judgements about what you're looking at or making plans for later, let go of your thoughts – just *be there*. This sounds so easy, but you probably won't find it easy to do at first. We're used to that internal commentary and it can be quite startling not to hear it, but it's also extremely restful.

Focus on your surroundings

This is a variation of doing nothing but it's somewhat easier. Again, sit down somewhere comfortable. Choose something in your surroundings, such as an item of furniture, a tree if you're looking into a garden, even some article of your clothing, and describe it to yourself in as much detail as you possibly can. Describe the colour and texture of the item, what it's made of, how old it may be. Continue this commentary for five minutes. This will sharpen your powers of concentration and observation.

Learn to use mindfulness, meditation or other similar mind–body techniques

These are more formal ways to help you practise staying in the present moment. They'll help you to increase your powers of concentration, and, as a result, you'll find you can pay attention more easily and more fully in other situations.

If such formal techniques don't appeal to you, you can still practise focusing on the moment. Choose a task that you find calming, such as taking a walk or weeding the garden. Make sure you concentrate fully, and only on that task. If your mind starts to wander into the future, or to rehash the past, simply bring your awareness back to what you're doing, to what's happening, *right now*.

Get into flow

The psychologist Mihalyi Csikszentmihalyi (see Chapter 8, Resources and Suggested Reading for details of his book) describes 'flow' as the feeling of being fully and completely engaged in what you're doing, unaware even of the passage of time. Artists and writers quite often describe this feeling once they've started developing an idea.

To find flow, you need to choose an activity that you enjoy, but that at the same time challenges you fully. Playing the piano, writing a poem, making an item of furniture, listening to music you love: these are the kinds of activities that encourage flow. If you take time to pursue hobbies or creative endeavours you love, you'll have an excellent chance of experiencing flow. The experience will leave you feeling calm and with a sense of fulfilment.

Myth 5: I must look perfect and stay that way

Overheard in the women's changing room at a sports club: 'I think I'll try some more Botox. I've found some new lines.' The reply from her friend was: 'Oh Sarah, not more treatment! Who do you think is going to win this race, you or Time?'

Perfection is a state, whereas living things change. No one, even if they were ever perfect once, can stay that way . . .

Furthermore, perfection is not as interesting as you might think. I will concede that the human eye is attracted to symmetry and there are a number of studies to support this. But much of what we consider to be attractive is judged to be so by its very imperfection. It's the little deviation, the slightly unexpected, that attracts the eye.

Of course, the real reason that lies behind our frantic race to look perfect is our fear of death. When we say perfect, we mean young. If we can continue to appear young, the thinking is, I suppose, that somehow we'll defy death. But this attitude only creates anxiety, because of course it's impossible not to die, and we all know it. The effort of pretending to win a race we know we're going to lose is exhausting and depressing.

It is, therefore, much easier to live a life that accepts change. Those individuals who identify the contribution that each stage of life brings – the refreshing innocence and energy of youth, the idealism and determination of young adulthood and the wisdom of later life – enjoy life more than those who fight change. Of course, no one enjoys the losses that ageing brings, but there are gains as well, and we tend to overlook them.

This doesn't mean that you have to let the grey show, or even that you must leave the wrinkles alone. As with everything in psychology, it's the intent that matters more than the act itself. What I'm suggesting here is simply that you accept the inevitable. Accept the facts that you will grow older and that you will die, and enjoy the precious time you have to live. Don't waste that precious time desperately pretending that death isn't going to happen. Those who accept the finiteness of life are more aware of its value, and can therefore enjoy it more fully.

So let's amend that fifth myth:

Perfection is actually rather boring. Each stage of life has value

SUGGESTIONS

Take care of the whole person
One of my patients devised this excellent way of valuing herself, rather than trying to change that self:

When her last child left home, Ellen, who is a talented artist, became depressed. When she was referred to me, she told me that she felt she'd lost all purpose. She'd stopped painting and was having enormous difficulty getting out of bed each day. She'd also begun to neglect herself and her home. I'd suggested a number of homework tasks for Ellen to try, but each one had seemed too large and daunting to her. She, however, came up with an excellent formula. She called it her 'mind/body/others' approach.

Ellen decided to set three tasks for herself each day: one to stimulate her mind, one to show she cared about her body and one to help someone else. She made sure that each task she set was modest, so that she could accomplish them all within a day. She set herself the goal of spending at least ten minutes on each activity: for example, looking at an art book (mind), putting on some make up (body), and ringing an elderly aunt to ask how she was (others). This balanced perspective helped her to regain a sense of herself.

As Ellen showed, it's important not to focus entirely on your appearance. We are so much more than simply how we look.

Focus on your strengths

This suggestion will be most powerful if you use mirror talk. Look in the mirror once each day and compliment yourself. Choose one positive thing to praise: perhaps you'd forgotten about that lovely dimple in your smile, or maybe you've been taking regular walks and your skin tone has improved. Start with yourself, but extend this to others as well. Offer a compliment – anything you can genuinely praise – to your partner or child, or a good friend, whenever possible. This focuses your awareness on what's pleasing, rather than on what isn't perfect. And don't limit yourself only to (narrow) physical attributes. Consider someone's thoughtfulness, or their sense of humour. Remember that there's much more to the self than the physical aspects.

Myth 6: I'll be happy when I'm rich and have all the latest products

Last year an old friend of mine sold the company he'd created. Having never been particularly well off before, he now has a lot, and I do mean a lot, of money. Recently we met up for a coffee, and I teased him 'So what have you been up to lately, now that you don't have to work?'

He didn't laugh. 'Well, I just got back from a two-week holiday with the family. We hired an entire island, and there was everything: beaches, swimming pool, chauffeur, the lot. After the first week, I found myself sitting in the bedroom one morning, my head splitting from the night before, sunburned, squinting out at the blazing sun, and thinking I just wanted to go home. It wasn't worth it.'

He's not the only wealthy person to feel less happy once he became rich than he did when he was less well off. Of course, there's a level of income below which life is indeed hard. However, above a basic amount, that is the money that's needed to supply you and your loved ones with all basic needs, there's little, if any, correlation between wealth and contentment. This is best illustrated in a study that was carried out by Daniel Kahneman and his colleagues at Princeton University (see Chapter 8, Resources and Suggested Reading). They questioned a large number of people who varied widely in the amount of money they earned. The researchers concluded that, in fact, income matters very little when it comes to how content people feel in their moment-to-moment experiences.

And don't be fooled into thinking that there's some specific, finite amount of money or goods that will guarantee to make you feel rich or to feel that you have all you'll ever want. The truth is, the more you have, the more you'll want. This is illustrated well in the fairy tale about the magic fish. In this story, a poor fisherman catches a talking fish. The fish begs the fisherman to set him free, offering to grant him any wish in exchange. The fisherman puts the fish back in the sea and hurries home to tell his wife. She asks for a fine house, and instantly they find themselves living in a fine house. The wife is happy for a time, but then tells her husband to go back to the sea and demand that the fish give them a castle instead. The fisherman obliges, and the couple at once find themselves the owners of a castle.

The castle, however, satisfies the wife for even less time than did the fine house. She then orders her husband to return to the sea and ask the fish that they become the king and queen of the land. The fisherman obliges. This goes on, with the wife calling for ever more, ever grander demands, and each time she remains satisfied for less time, until finally the magic fish gets fed up and returns the couple to their humble cottage, because it's clear that nothing would ever be enough for her.

In his book, *Richistan: A Journey Through the 21st Century Wealth Boom and the Lives of the New Rich* (see Chapter 8, Resources and Suggested Reading), Robert Frank explores the theory that riches only make you hungrier for more. He asked a number of super-rich people how much money they'd need to feel secure. Whatever they earned, they told Frank, they would need approximately twice as much as they had at the present time before they would feel secure.

Furthermore, when you have a lot you become needier than when you didn't have so much. You don't believe me? Listen to these wise words from *The Prophet*:

For what are your possessions but things you keep and
    guard for fear you may need them tomorrow?
And tomorrow, what shall tomorrow bring to the

over-prudent dog burying bones in the trackless sand as
he follows the pilgrims to the holy city?
And what is fear of need but need itself?
Is not dread of thirst when your well is full, the thirst
that is unquenchable?

Or, in more modern terminology: the more you have, the
more you must insure, guard, alarm, protect with tracking
devices, and worry about losing.

It's very hard, I know, to believe that you could be happier
with less, when you're bombarded relentlessly by advertisements suggesting that you need to buy this, and borrow for
that. Things that are really only wants are cleverly packaged
by their manufacturers to appear as needs. The companies
that do this are not doing so because they want you to be
happy. Quite the opposite, they want you to need what they're
selling so that they can make a profit by using you. And they
don't want you to be satisfied for long. They want you to
need something more as soon as possible, so they can make
more profit.

Our entire economy is based on all of us buying more and
more, whether we need it or not. We aren't even given the
dignity of being referred to as people any more, let alone as
individuals. Nowadays we're grouped together as consumers
and customers. The emphasis is on what we can take in and
use up, it seems, rather than what we can contribute or share,
or how we might enjoy what we already have.

There's a lovely Chinese story that illustrates this point
well. A poor farmer and his wife have just had their third
child, and it's now too crowded in their little house. So the
husband goes to the wise man in the village and asks him
for advice. The wise man suggests to the farmer that he brings
his farmyard animals into the house. He's surprised, but, after
all, this is the wise man speaking and so he goes home and
does as he's been told.

But now the situation is even worse, of course. It's more crowded in the house than ever before. The farmer and his wife can hardly move without tripping over someone or something. They bear the situation for several weeks, but then, in desperation, the husband returns to the wise man and asks for further advice. The wise man suggests that he moves the farmyard animals out of the house. Now of course, there seems to be plenty of room, and the farmer and his wife and his children are content once more, even though nothing has really changed.

The wise man knew that this man couldn't afford a bigger house. He therefore decided to help him find a way to accept that what he had already was adequate.

We can now reword the sixth myth:

Money alone won't make me happy. Taking the time to enjoy what I already have will bring me contentment

SUGGESTIONS

Distinguish between needs and wants

Oliver James talks about this eloquently in his recent book *Affluenza* (see Chapter 8, Resources and Suggested Reading). Because our economy only thrives if we continue to buy more and more goods, businesses make a point of blurring the line between needs and wants. Our basic needs – adequate food, warmth and shelter – should be the priority, unless, that is, we listen to advertisers. It's difficult to know, for example, how many items of clothing a person 'needs' nowadays, or what foods are 'necessary'. And we're further confused by terms such as 'must-haves' and 'spend and save'. The best way to keep your perspective is to drop the terms 'need' and 'want' altogether. Just list everything that you spend your money on. Then put that list in order of priority. At the top go the items that ensure you continue to stay well, go about your daily routines and go to work or school. Next are the items you could do without, but that you'd miss. Last are the items that you purchase solely because of social or commercial pressure. This list will help you to decide what to spend your money on.

Understand money

Money is the triumph of belief over logic. Money consists of bits of plastic, pieces of paper and pieces of common metals. Yet because we've been told that these things are valuable, we believe that money can make us strong and powerful. Money has become an end in itself, when actually it's only a symbol that we're asked to value.

I have a friend who's immensely wealthy, and she married into another immensely wealthy family, so there's more money than can be counted. She has everything I could ever imagine having, she's constantly surrounded by admirers and she's always being asked to parties and other social occasions. Yet, she often tells me that she feels lonely.

I found this hard to understand, so I once asked her how she can feel lonely when so many people want to spend time with her. She looked at me rather sadly and said 'I'm always looking for people who want to be with *me*, rather than with what I have. I've developed a sort of sixth sense about it, and I can tell who's who. The sad thing is, I hardly ever meet anyone who wants me just for me.'

Money can isolate you and make you feel lonely, and it also makes you more needy. People who have lots of money tend to buy lots of things, and, as I pointed out earlier in this chapter, the more things you have, the more must be kept safe. In effect, then, the more you have the needier you become.

This isn't to say that money and happiness can never go together. I'm sure there are some wealthy people who are happy. Usually, however, they're happiest when they're sharing their wealth rather than guarding it, as Scrooge would no doubt tell you.

If you treat money and material goods as if they are ends in themselves, you'll never know contentment. As masters, money and material goods are like drugs, and all you'll want is more of them. Use your material wealth as means to your ends, rather than as ends in themselves.

Myth 7: I'll be happy once I'm famous and have achieved goals that other people find impressive

In truth, the great achievements, or even the awards and medals and applause they may bring, give little lasting satisfaction. What's absorbing and enjoyable are the steps along the way to achievement – that is, the journey itself rather than the destination.

This is exactly what's meant by flow. I've already described flow briefly earlier in this chapter, but here's a fuller description (see Chapter 8, Resources and Suggested Reading) from Howard Gardner, a colleague of Mihalyi Csikszentmihalyi:

In flow we feel totally involved, lost in a seemingly effortless performance. Paradoxically, we feel 100 per cent alive when we are so committed to the task at hand that we lose track of time, of our interests – even of our own existence. Intense flow can happen anywhere: in making love, in listening to music, in playing a good game of squash or chess.

In other words, optimal experience occurs while you're working on something that's important to you, much more so than after you achieve a goal or when you're taking a break from your efforts. Remember, then, when you set your goals, not to worry about the endpoint so much as the process. If what you choose is fun, and if it stretches your abilities and adds to what you know, you'll be happy.

So let's replace that seventh myth with this amendment:

My greatest fulfilment will come while I'm engaged in activities that are important and enjoyable to me, and that challenge me

SUGGESTIONS

Rediscover your early interests
It's said that we are most true to ourselves, that is, the least influenced by others, when we're about nine or ten years old. At that age, we're independent and capable enough not to need the constant attention of our parents. At the same time, we've not yet entered puberty, and so are not yet driven to seek the approval and intimacy of our peers. Nine to ten is a good age, therefore, to discover your own real interests.

What did you most enjoy at that age? How did you spend your free time? Could you pick up, or adapt those interests now? They may well offer you the chance to experience flow.

Have as many hobbies or projects on the go as you like
Remember, it's the process of doing that counts not any creation that results from it (although you may be very satisfied with anything you do create). Therefore, feel free to chase as many of your interests and enthusiasms as you like in your free time. This is particularly important for those of you who have a job that demands completed projects or reports with

hard-and-fast deadlines. The release of simply exploring your interests will, in itself, feel therapeutic.

Spend some time each week on activities that have no purpose other than to be enjoyable

Even if you only have half an hour a week, be sure you have some time to play. As we saw in Chapter 1, today's emphasis on being busy doesn't allow enough time for play. This in turn means we're not allowing time to be genuinely creative. Creativity, like flow, encourages a sense of contentment.

CASE STUDY: Caroline

Caroline arrived for her first appointment with me looking like she was ready for a photo shoot, Her clothes were tailored and expensive, her hair was carefully cut and coloured, and her makeup was perfect. She looked much younger than her 45 years.

Caroline had previously been to see her GP because she'd begun to have panic attacks at work. On two occasions, she'd felt so anxious that she'd had to cancel appointments with key clients because she was convinced that she would faint during the consultations.

Her GP had ordered some tests to check her physical health, and he'd then prescribed a course of antidepressants, but Caroline stopped taking them after only one week because she said that they made her think too slowly. The GP then suggested that she try cognitive-behaviour therapy. Caroline refused initially, but when the frequency of the panic attacks began to increase, she agreed to give it a try.

It was clear when Caroline entered the consulting room that she'd been anxiously hyperventilating while she was waiting. Throughout our time together, she glanced continually at her watch and checked her mobile, and she had difficulty sitting still, shifting restlessly. At one point she asked if I would open the window because she told me that she needed more air.

As soon as she entered the room, Caroline informed me that she would have to leave five minutes early because she needed to be back in the office in time for an important meeting. She added that if we were going to work together, it was imperative that she missed as little work as possible, because any loss of income would be a serious concern. She had come along, she added, only because the GP had been so insistent.

She said that her panic attacks had started two months earlier, and that she was convinced that they'd come out of the blue. However, when we talked about what was happening at that time in her life, she admitted that they coincided roughly with the time when her son, Alex, had started applying to go to university.

At this point in the interview, and to her own surprise, Caroline became tearful. She said that when her son had started to choose the university he wanted to go to, she'd realised that she was about to lose her only child, and that she felt as if she'd hardly seen him during the last few years.

Alex had been conceived within a year of her going off the pill, and his birth had been straightforward. Caroline had stayed at home with him as a full-time mum during the first two years of his life, which she described as 'the happiest time of my life'. However, a friend in the law firm where she was now a partner had told her about a position coming up that was 'just too lucrative to pass up', and she'd gone back to work full time just as Alex had his third birthday.

Caroline told me that she and her husband had always intended to have another child, and she'd simply assumed that it would be as easy as it had been the first time. Her husband, Adrian, was also a solicitor. He worked in a large firm in a neighbouring city some 30 miles away. They both worked extremely long hours, and often went in to work at the weekend. 'Somehow,' she said ,'it just never seemed the right moment to get pregnant again.'

Therefore, she and Adrian had been determined, instead, to give Alex every opportunity that a child can have. He attended an exclusive public school, and was involved in numerous extra-curricular activities; and the family took at least two foreign holidays every year.

Caroline's parents had been very ambitious for both of their daughters, who went to public schools, and had been involved in a number of activities outside of school as well. These opportunities came at a great financial sacrifice to her parents, 'as we were continually reminded' Caroline told me a bit ruefully. She described her sister, three years her junior, as 'the sporty one', although Caroline herself loved dancing and had achieved a high standard in ballet.

Both sisters went on to university and both trained professionally. Caroline qualified as a solicitor and her sister as a GP. Both were now married. Her sister worked part time and had three daughters. Caroline described her as 'more laid back than I am'.

She described her parents, on the other hand, as 'highly strung'. They were still together and both were now retired. Her mother had worked part time as a secretary for a firm of solicitors, and her father had had a number of jobs, although 'none for very long . . . He was a restless man,' Caroline told me. He'd been made redundant once when Caroline was five, and although he'd found work again within a year, she told me that her parents had never stopped talking about this event.

I asked Caroline if she'd ever considered reducing the number of hours she worked so that she'd have more time to relax and to be at home. She seemed annoyed by this, saying, 'I thought you'd suggest something like that. I couldn't possibly reduce my hours. In fact, I'm not sure how we're going to manage as it is, now that Alex is going off to university.'

Caroline insisted that if we were to meet, we must restrict our work together to six sessions, and to devote them only to helping her get rid of her panicky feelings. This we did, employing several of the suggestions from Chapter 3. Within four sessions her anxiety was greatly reduced. Her success had also encouraged her to look beyond symptom relief, and start to find ways of preventing her anxiety levels spiralling upwards in the first place.

During our work together, Caroline had begun to recognise some of her 'should' statements, particularly with regard to the long hours she worked, and to let go of them. She was also relaxing more often. By the sixth session, she admitted that she was quite pleased with the changes in her lifestyle and her way of thinking, and we agreed that we would stop meeting.

Eight months later, however, Caroline rang me. Could she see me again? She told me that she'd been thinking a lot about what we'd discussed, and that she now wanted to take things a step further. She accepted the first appointment time I offered her; and I was pleased to note that she didn't specify that our meeting had to be either during her lunch hour or that she had to have the last appointment of the day.

Caroline started the session by telling me that a great deal had happened during the eight months. Alex had been accepted by the three universities he'd applied to, and he was greatly looking forward to starting his course at the one he had chosen, in a few months' time. Caroline had taken time off work 'almost without thinking about it and certainly without feeling guilty about it', she said with pride. She was able to take Alex to visit the universities, and she said she'd enjoyed enormously watching him choose the one he wanted to attend. 'This would never have happened if I hadn't started resetting my priorities,' she added.

She explained that the reason she'd wanted to see me again was that she'd realised that some of her beliefs weren't helping her to feel satisfied or happy 'So many things I thought we needed – that Alex needed in particular – I now realise that we don't need at all. In fact, some of it, all those foreign touring holidays in particular, none of us really even enjoyed that much!

'I also realised how ridiculous it is that I try to look like I'm 30 or something,' she went on. 'I mean, the thing I'm most proud of is that I'm a mother. And my son is now grown! It's silly to try to look like I'm still 30!' She loved looking good, she explained, but now she could see how different that was from looking as young and as perfect as possible.

Obviously, releasing herself from the expensive holidays and the numerous age-fighting beauty treatments that she routinely underwent meant that Caroline was now spending a great deal less money. 'The reason I've come to see you again is that I think I'm ready to explore the idea of working part time. But this is the very time in my life when I thought I would want to step up my work! So I'd like some help adjusting to that. I was hoping you could help me use my new-found free time to feel happier and more relaxed, rather than just to get busy in other ways.'

We started talking about what part time would mean for her. We decided that, if it was possible, a gradual reduction in her working hours was preferable to a sudden change; she agreed to discuss this matter with the other partners.

Caroline wasn't sure herself what she meant by part-time work, so I suggested that she start by looking through her finances to determine what her minimum salary could be. She also agreed to do nothing for two minutes every evening, or to practise mindfulness each day, so she could start introducing herself to the idea of having unstructured time.

When she came back for her next session, it was with good news. Her partners had agreed that she could reduce her hours in stages, as long as she gave a three-month notice of any reduction. They were sorry that she would be working less, but they'd given her their full backing.

Caroline's budgeting surprised her. She'd discovered that, now that the family didn't wish to travel so much and she was spending less on herself, she could in fact cut her hours by half. However, at the same time, she felt that this was too drastic for a first step.

She told me that she'd also begun to worry about how she'd spend her new free time. She was afraid of becoming panicky without what she called 'a clear purpose'. Even though she wanted the freedom, she also was afraid of it. I suggested that she might start by setting small goals, without any grand purpose, simply as an experiment, so that she could see how it felt for her to spend time in a less directed way. We agreed that for a first reduction she'd work four days a week. On the fifth day each week, she'd practise the 'mind/body/others' suggestion that Ellen had used so successfully (see page 141) and passed on to me.

During the three-month notice period before her first reduction in working hours, Caroline also agreed to talk to family members and to look back at old diaries, so that she could discover her hobbies and interests when she was at primary school, and, in particular, when she was nine or ten years old.

Four months later, we met again. Caroline was still very smartly turned out, but now she looked much happier and more relaxed. She said she was definitely enjoying her day off work each week. However, to her own surprise and delight, she found that she resented making any plans on her free day. Even the mind/body/other technique made her day feel too restricted, so she'd dropped it to leave the day unplanned.

She told me that what pleased her most was that she no longer felt panicky, either at home or at work, when she had free time. 'If I get a break at work, I don't look immediately for something to fill in the time. I do some paced breathing, or I take a longer lunch break.'

Caroline's investigations into her childhood had reminded her how much she'd loved dancing. As a result, she had decided to enrol in an adult dancing class. She and her husband had also bought tickets to several ballet performances; and they had also visited Alex at university, where he seemed very settled and happy.

Caroline was unsure about whether she'd want to reduce her working hours even further. 'I've decided to leave things for another three months, and then I'll think again,' she told me. That decision in itself was important; she happily conceded that a year ago, she could not have simply left her options open. A year ago, she would have insisted on making a plan first, but this new flexible, more open approach was allowing her to enjoy life much more.

How this applies to you

I chose Caroline as the case study in this chapter, although she could easily have been my choice in Chapter 3 on anxiety. I did so because Caroline had the determination and foresight to look beyond her immediate difficulties, and the courage to admit that her outlook accounted in large part for her anxiety in the first place.

This may well be so for you, too. Once you're sleeping well, or once you're feeling calmer and more positive and can concentrate on what's going on around you, you're quite likely to realise that you're holding on to one or more of the myths and that it, or they, will continue to sabotage your peace of mind unless you do something about it. That's the time to take up some of the suggestions in this chapter.

As Caroline has showed us so well, learning how to be content isn't something that you 'sort out' in one stroke – it's a process, an evolution. Development never proceeds in a simple straight line. Remember, as Gibran says so wisely in *The Prophet,* 'The soul unfolds itself, like a lotus of countless petals.'

7

Relapse

*The soul walks not upon a line, neither does it grow
like a reed. The soul unfolds itself, like a lotus of
countless petals.*

The Prophet
Kahlil Gibran

I often wonder why so little has been written about relapse.
Perhaps it makes psychologists feel uncomfortable. Perhaps
we feel we've failed our patients in some way if they relapse.

Actually, it's incredibly common to relapse, in the sense
that it's incredibly common to drift back towards old habits,
or to react in old ways when you're under stress. It's so
common, in fact, that I'm sure it's safe to say that it's normal
to have relapses. So why, then, do we all feel such failures
when they happen?

I think it's because most of us have bought into the
modern misconception that, psychologically, you develop in
a straight line. We've already talked about the fact that life
doesn't proceed logically, nor does it always make sense
at the time. It's also unrealistic to assume that whenever
we make a mistake, we correct it and move on without a
backward glance. This oversimplified model ignores the
complicated role of motivation when we choose how to react.

It ignores the power of habit. It ignores the role that person-ality traits such as impulsiveness play in determining our behaviours. It ignores the fact that learning a lesson in one context may not teach us enough to decide what to do in similar contexts.

So, please start this chapter by dropping the negative connotations from the term 'relapse'. Let's just call it 'change in an undesired direction', shall we?

Whenever you sense that you're falling back into old habits and they're not doing you any good, what you need to do is to stop, reconsider and then redirect yourself. I'll show you how to do so in this chapter. Relapse is a time for action, but there's simply no need for recriminations.

If you've followed the spirit of this book, you'll have collected and kept baseline diaries of your problems, as well as notes about which suggestions, challenges and amend-ments have helped you most. You'll also have written down how you've altered the suggestions, challenges and amend-ments to suit you. You're already well on your way to sorting out any relapses you may have.

I can't stress strongly enough the importance of keeping written records. If you do this as you go along, it saves you having to start all over again when you find yourself drifting back towards the old unhappy ways of thinking and behaving. Instead of making an entirely new start, you'll only need to dig out your diaries and notes to remind yourself of exactly what's previously worked for you.

I work with my patients in this way. In the first session, each one is given a notebook, which then gradually becomes his or her personalised treatment manual or Relapse Survival Guide. To create your own manual, you'll want to include a definition of each of your problems, a list of suggestions, challenges and amendments (include those that worked for you as well as those that didn't) and regular summaries of your progress. You can write all of this out each time that you feel you've identified and sorted a problem successfully, or you can do this periodically whenever you have time.

Relapse survival guide – definitions

Before you can decide how to help yourself, you need to know clearly what the problem is, and how bad it is. If you've been following the suggestions in this book, you'll have started doing this already. If you're suffering from a sleep disturbance, anxiety or a tendency to panic, you'll have kept a baseline diary (see Chapters 2 and 3). If your problem is a tendency to dwell on an unhappy past, you'll have identified which suggestions help you to let go of your anger and resentment (see Chapter 4). If negative thinking or a loss of contentment is your problem, you'll have a good idea of the unhelpful beliefs that have supported your maladaptive thinking (see Chapter 5).

However, what if your relapse concerns a problem that you worked on before you read this book, or what if it's one that you solved without following the methods I've described here? In that case, you could try to construct the relevant definitions now, although I must caution you that this won't be as accurate as collecting the information at the time.

Therefore, if you've not used this book to help you sort out a particular problem that's now recurred, it would probably be better to approach it as if you're now troubled by it for the first time. Refer to the appropriate chapters and treat the problem as if it's a new one.

When gathering information in their notebooks, my patients leave a blank page after defining each problem and gathering the information for a baseline. Then during our final session, we use that page to summarise the problem as accurately and as precisely as possible.

Let me give you some examples from the case studies:

Rose

With regard to her sleep problem, Rose wrote this:

> It took me about 70 minutes to fall asleep when I first got into bed. I woke between four and eight times during the night, and I usually needed about an hour and a half to fall asleep again. Despite spending ten or 11 hours in bed, my average sleeping time each night was only four hours.

Helen

When Helen defined anxiety, she wrote this:

> At my worst, four out of every five of my thoughts were about what I should do for other people. I was aware of these worries at some level all the time. I rated my anxiety levels as never less than 40 per cent, and often as 80 per cent or even higher. At 80 per cent I thought I might panic. The anxiety was lowest when I was seeing patients or reading to my children, and highest when I first tried to go to sleep at night.

Martin

Defining his negative beliefs, Martin wrote:

> I weighed 14 stone when I first started therapy. I was convinced that my weight and age alone would be the basis on which others would judge me, and that no one would find me acceptable company. I believed this, despite the fact that I realised I had some true friends. I was also convinced that everyone except me had a loving partner.

Now, having looked back to see just how bad things once were, many of you will be feeling better already. You'll be able to see from your summaries that things have been as bad, or even worse in the past. Remember, too, that despite this, you managed to make impressive improvements. You can do it again, and this time, you can do it more quickly.

What worked and what didn't

The next step is to study your notes to find out which suggestions, challenges and amendments have helped you feel better and behave more adaptively.

During our last session, many of my patients choose to write a 'prescription' in their notebooks. This prescription includes the suggestions, challenges and amendments that helped them the most, as well as those that didn't work so well. They can then refer to this prescription when they sense they're about to relapse, or have already done so.

Examples of prescriptions

Let's look again at our three examples, to see what they wrote down as their own prescriptions:

Rose

My birdsong tape helps me get to sleep when I first get into bed.

If I wake during the night, I need to go to my retreat, drink some sweet tea, and work on my scrapbooks, or read a romantic novel, until I feel tired. It's fine to do this as often as I need to because I'll feel more rested the next day, not less.

The 'relaxation tapes' I can buy don't work for me very well, so I need to use only my birdsong tapes.

I need to be strict about a regular routine each night, and make sure that it includes a shower and a regular bedtime of ten o'clock.

Helen

If I wake at night with worries on my mind, I'll transfer them to my worry list. If I'm still worrying I can brainstorm and write myself a 'to do' list for the next day. Then I can forget about them. Mindfulness or paced breathing will help me to fall asleep again.

If I find myself worrying, or thinking 'should' thoughts during the day, 40 paced breaths help me to forget about them. For the next few days I'll also need to set my alarm five minutes earlier in the morning and start each day with 40 paced breaths.

It's also important for me to make sure that I allow time to have three or four sessions of aerobic exercise, each for at least 20 minutes, every week.

Martin

My ideal weight is between 12 and 13 stone.

I can lose weight successfully at the rate of about a pound a week, if I attend Weight Watchers regularly. I feel good when I'm following the Weight Watchers diet, and feeling good is more important than achieving a specific weight.

Meditation and regular walks calm my mind. I'm most likely to remember to meditate if I attend classes regularly.

I now realise that I'm not the only single person among my friends.

When I talk to other people, I'm most relaxed when I'm asking them to tell me about themselves.

It's important for me always to listen carefully to other

people. For me, listening carefully is a type of mindfulness and it helps me feel calmer, and, also, more accepted by others.

A new baseline

As soon as you're aware that you're relapsing, start keeping a new (and modified) baseline. Remember, this is the best way to accumulate accurate information about what triggers your problem.

Record each relevant occasion: the nights you slept poorly, the occasions when you registered anxiety in your discomfort zone, the moments when you caught yourself turning over negative and discouraging thoughts – in other words, whenever the problem you've identified occurs. Make a note of when this occurred, where you were, what else was happening, who you were with and any other factors you suspect may be relevant. If you prefer, you can use the template I've included overleaf.

Keep this baseline long enough to record at least five examples of your problem. Next, summarise what you believe to be the triggers that set off your problematic behaviour.

The new prescription

If the triggers you've identified are the same ones that you've dealt with before, you may be able to use your original prescription without having to modify it. If, as is more likely, you've identified some new triggers, you'll need to write out a prescription so you can deal with them. Basically, there are two approaches you can take:

Baseline relapse diary

Date: Day:

Time				
The possible relapse, thought(s), negative belief(s), myths or unhelpful behaviour(s)				
Where was I?				
With whom?				
Doing what?				
Any thoughts				
Any other information				
What worked when I first sorted this problem?				
What other suggestions could I try?				
Suggestions tried (if relevant)				
How successful? (% optional)				

1 Avoid the triggers that cause relapse

Say, for example, that you've been feeling depressed and discouraged in the mornings – something you'd not experienced for over a year. Your baseline diary shows that you've started listening to a particular news programme during breakfast. It's very easy for this to affect your mood so simply stop listening to that news bulletin, or change the time of day that you listen to news.

2 Try some new suggestions if the triggers can't be avoided

Let's say you're waking up feeling very depressed and upset in the morning because you're having nightmares. You could try doing five minutes of paced breathing as soon as you wake, and use a thought blocker while you're getting ready for your day, so there's no opportunity to think about the nightmares. Or you could listen to the radio at that time (but preferably *not* to a radio station that broadcasts disaster-laden news!).

Once you've found some suggestions that help, write out a revised daily prescription for the next three weeks (three weeks, remember, is about the right amount of time needed to break a habit). It's wise to include in this prescription a daily session of 40 paced breaths or five minutes of mindfulness on waking, and to set yourself a regular bedtime. If you can start your day calmly, and if you can try to get adequate rest, you're more likely to overcome your problem.

Keep your notebook where you can refer to it easily every day, and keep a written record of what works for you and what doesn't.

An added extra

You can encourage a positive outlook if you choose to include one uplifting activity in your schedule each day. This needn't take much time; even five minutes will help. You may find some suggestions in your original notes, or look at the suggestions throughout the book, particularly those we looked at in Chapter 6.

Some ideas

To give you some ideas, here's what Rose, Helen and Martin chose:

Rose

She chose to take a walk with her husband each evening, which was the time of day when she felt at her lowest. This made her feel more alert and energised. She also made sure that she commented to her husband about something beautiful that she noticed during the walk.

Helen

She started her day with five minutes of mindfulness, and set aside ten minutes each evening to do some yoga. This helped her to relax on a regular basis.

Martin

He treated himself to some new DVDs to watch in the evenings when he, too, felt at his lowest. He also signed up to attend Weight Watchers again, and to ask questions and listen carefully to others during the meetings.

Accessories

Remember also to make use of any props that have helped you:

Rose found her birdsong tapes and her scrapbooks and photos.

Helen bought a yoga book that her teacher had recommended.

Martin got hold of some films he'd been wanting to watch.

Mirror talk

Finally, and this is really important, use mirror talk to praise yourself each day for taking these positive steps. This will encourage you to carry on with your new habits, and remind you that your renewed efforts will also help to rebuild your self-esteem.

Review

At the end of three weeks, summarise how you're feeling in your notebook. Write down the progress you've made, remembering to be as specific as you can in case you need to refer to this information in the future.

If you think this three-week focus has turned you around, you can put everything away safely. If you think you still have a way to go, set yourself another three-week prescription and continue monitoring your progress. I've found that most of my patients need about six weeks of refocusing before they feel they're no longer in danger of relapsing.

I think you'll find this personalised approach to problem solving far more helpful than any off-the-peg approach. Furthermore, the fact that you manage to regain a balanced outlook on life will add to your self-esteem. Problems are a normal part of life, and each time you overcome a problem, you'll have learned more about yourself, and about how to make your life happier, richer and more fulfilling.

Remember, things can always improve.

Resources and Suggested Reading

In this chapter, I've included the resources and references that I consulted in writing this book. I've also included the works that I most frequently suggest to my own patients to read as a part of their homework assignments. The books and articles are listed in alphabetical order, and after each one I'll describe briefly the problems and the issues that I think it handles particularly well.

Resources

General

BBC
www.bbc.co.uk

This is a large general site. If you click on 'Health' and then 'Healthy living', you'll be directed to sites that contain helpful factsheets about good nutrition and appropriate exercise, and on anxiety and panics, insomnia and relaxation techniques.

Mind
www.mind.org.uk

This is another general website, with well written factsheets about anxiety, panic attacks, sleep problems, yoga and relaxation. If you wish to speak to someone in your area, click on 'Mind in your area' and fill in your post code.

Royal College of Psychiatrists
17 Belgrave Square
London
SW1X 8PG
Tel: 0207 2352351
www.rcpsych.ac.uk

The website contains detailed and well written factsheets, particularly about anxiety and phobias and about sleep problems.

British Association for Behavioural and Cognitive Psychotherapies (BABCP)
Victoria Buildings
9–13 Silver Street
Bury
BL9 0EU
Tel: 0161 7974484
www.babcp.com

This site has in particular a well written factsheet about anxiety, and there's a site to help you find a Cognitive Behaviour therapist.

British Psychological Society (BPS)
St. Andrew's House
48 Princess Road East
Leicester
LE1 7DR
Tel: 0116 2549568
www.bps.org.uk/public

The BPS has probably the most comprehensive site for finding a therapist, and they are now developing a series of factsheets on topics such as anxiety and panics.

British Association for Counselling and Psychotherapy (BACP)
BACP House
15 St. John's Business Park
Lutterworth
LE17 4HB
Tel: 0870 4435252
www.bacp.co.uk

This site has a 'find a therapist' service.

BUPA
www.bupa.co.uk

This is a private health care company, but in addition to offering private health care, they offer a series of well written factsheets on their website. Particularly good are the factsheets on anxiety disorders, phobias and insomnia.

NHS Direct
www.nhsdirect.nhs.uk

This site is slanted towards physical health, but there are factsheets on anxiety, panic disorder and insomnia.

Sleep Disturbance

BBC
www.bbc.co.uk

For sleep problems, go to
www.bbc.co.uk/health/conditions/insomnia.

Mind
www.mind.org.uk

Click on 'sleep problems'.

Royal College of Psychiatrists
www.rcpsych.ac.uk

Under 'mental health information', click on 'sleep problems'.

BUPA
www.bupa.co.uk

Click on 'insomnia'.

NHS Direct.
www.nhsdirect.nhs.uk

Click on 'insomnia'.

Anxiety and Panic Attacks

BBC
www.bbc.co.uk

For help with anxiety and panic attacks, go to www.bbc.co.uk/health/conditions/mentalhealth/anxietydisorders. For 'anxiety disorders' you can substitute 'phobias and panic attacks'.

Mind
www.mind.org.uk

Click on 'anxiety' or 'panic attacks'.

British Association for Behavioural and Cognitive Psychotherapies (BABCP)
www.bacp.co.uk

Click on 'anxiety'.

Royal College of Psychiatrists
www.rcpsych.ac.uk

Click on 'anxiety and phobias'.

BUPA
www.bupa.co.uk

Click on 'anxiety disorders' and on 'phobias'.

NHS Direct
www.nhsdirect.nhs.uk

Click on 'anxiety' and 'panic disorder'.

Triumph Over Phobias (TOP UK)
www.topuk.org

Describes the sort of help you might want to look for and recommends reading material and related websites.

Mindfulness and Relaxation Techniques

BBC
www.bbc.co.uk

Go to www.bbc.co.uk/health/conditions/mentalhealth/
relaxation

Mind
www.mind.org.uk

Go to 'stress' for a guide to relaxation, and to 'complementary therapies' for information about yoga.

Centre for Mindfulness Research Practice
School of Psychology
Dean Street Building
Bangor University
Bangor
LL57 1UT
Tel: 01248 382939
www.bangor.ac.uk/imscar/mindfulness

This organisation offers courses on mindfulness as well as books and articles, tapes and CDs.

The Mayo Clinic
www.mayoclinic.com/health/relaxation-techniques

This factsheet describes the benefits of relaxation and offers various types of relaxation.

British Wheel of Yoga
BWY
Central Office
25 Jermyn Street
Sleaford
Lincs
NG34 7RU
Tel: 01529 306851
www.bwy.org.uk

Social Networking

Friends Reunited
www.friendsreunited.co.uk

Wikipedia
http://wikipedia.org/

For a list of frequently accessed social networking sites, go to
Wikipedia, and then 'list of social networking sites'.

Healthy Living

BBC
www.bbc.co.uk

For information on nutrition, go to
www.bbc.co.uk/health/healthyliving/nutrition; for information on fitness, substitute 'fitness' for 'nutrition'.

Mind
www.mind.org.uk

Click on 'food and mood' and on 'physical activity'.

Alexander Technique
Society of Teachers of the Alexander Technique (STAT)
1st floor
Linton House
39–51 Highgate Road
London
NW5 1RS
Tel: 0207 4825135
www.stat.org.uk

The Alexander Technique is a way of breathing and carrying yourself so that your body is in its most natural position. The site has a directory of qualified teachers.

Books and articles

Barker, Sarah, *The Alexander Technique*, Bantam Books Inc., 1990.
(The author offers a number of relaxation and calming techniques. It's very practical.)

Beck, Aaron T., *Cognitive Therapy and the Emotional Disorders*, Penguin Books, 1991.
(This book describes negative thinking and its role in maintaining low mood. The style is fairly academic.)

Beck, Aaron T., Rush, A. John, Shaw, Brian F., and Emery, Gary, *Cognitive Therapy of Depression*, The Guildford Press, 1987.
(The authors present a detailed picture of negative thinking and depression. As before, Beck's style is fairly academic.)

Biddulph, Steve, *Raising Babies: why your love is best*, Harper/Thorsons, 2006.

(Biddulph describes the importance of early experience. The style is very down to earth.)

Blair, L., 'Parents right to allow small freedoms for 10-year-olds', *The Times*, 10 August 2002.

(This was my attempt to put some perspective into a tragic news story.)

Briggs, Harold E., *Complete Poetry and Selected Prose of Keats*, Random House, 1967.

(I used the quote about youth, from 'Ode on a Grecian Urn', p. 295, in Chapter Six.)

Bristol, Claude M., *The Magic of Believing*, Prentice-Hall, Inc., 1977.

(Bristol celebrates the power of positive thinking. He describes how to use positive self-talk and positive imagery. It's a practical guide, but the examples are somewhat dated.)

Bruner, J.S., Jolly, A., and Sylva, K. (eds), *Play: its role in development and evolution*, Penguin Books, 1976.

(The quote I've used in Chapter 1 is taken from article by Erik Erikson, 'Play and Actuality', pp. 688–704, quote on p. 691. This lovely book is comprised of articles by many authors, from many perspectives about the meaning and importance of play.)

Covey, Stephen, *The Seven Habits of Highly Effective People*, Simon & Schuster, 1999.

(Covey offers a number of methods to encourage positive thinking, and gives practical suggestions about how to organise yourself and improve your effectiveness.)

Csikszentmihalyi, M., *Flow: The Classic Work on How to Achieve Happiness*, Rider & Co., 2002.

(The author helps you understand what it really means to become truly involved with what you love to do.)

De Botton, A., *Status Anxiety*, Penguin Books, 2004.

(De Botton discusses the ways that current cultural attitudes contribute to our loss of contentment. It's beautifully written.)

Dalai Lama, H.H. and Cutler, Howard, *The Art of Happiness*, Hodder & Stoughton, 1999.
(This is a careful and detailed look at what happiness means, which is not quite the same as contentment, so it makes for some helpful comparisons.)

Dickens, Charles, *A Christmas Carol*, Hazell, Watson and Viney Ltd, 1868.
(Scrooge tells us how money doesn't buy happiness.)

Dominguez, Joe and Robin, Vicki, *Your Money or Your Life*, Penguin Books, 1992.
(The authors explain what money is all about, and how to keep it from controlling you. They offer sensible suggestions about how to budget, and novel ways to think about your work.)

Dowden, Edward (ed.), *The Histories and Poems of William Shakespeare*, Oxford University Press, 1912.
(I quote from Shakespeare's twenty-fifth sonnet, p. 361, Chapter 6.)

Dowden, Edward (ed.), *The Tragedies of William Shakespeare*, Oxford University Press, 1912.
(I use the quote from *Hamlet*, Act II scene ii, p. 300 at the beginning of Chapter 5.)

Earle, Richard, Imrie, David, Archbold, Rick, *Your Vitality Factor*, Pan Macmillan, 1991.
(This books defines stress clearly, and offers a number of questionnaires you can use to help sort out your priorities and find ways to overcome stress. It contains lots of practical advice.)

Ellis, Albert, *Human Psychotherapy: The Rational-emotive Approach*, McGraw-Hill, 1973.
(Ellis offers a number of suggestions for overcoming negative thinking.)

Erikson, Erik H., 'Identity and the Lifecycle', Monograph, *Psychological Issues*, vol. I, no. 1, International Universities Press, 1959.

(The author describes how we continue to grow and change throughout life, and not just in childhood.)

Estes, Clarissa Pinkola, *Women Who Run with the Wolves*, Random House, 1992.
(In this beautifully written book, Estes uses fairy tales and legends to describe some of the eternal issues that concern women.)

Fitzgerald, Edward (trans.), *The Rubáiyát of Omar Khayyám*, Dover Publications, 1995.
(I use the quote about time, p. 15, at the beginning of Chapter 4.)

First, Michael B., *Diagnostic and Statistical Manual of Mental Disorders*, fourth ed., American Psychiatric Association, 1994.
(This is a very academic book. It contains clear descriptions of mental disorders. I used this throughout my work, but particularly to write Chapters 2 and 3.)

Frank, Robert, *Richistan: A Journey Through the 21st Century Wealth Boom and the Lives of the New Rich*, Piatkus, 2007.
(Wall Street Journal reporter Robert Frank explores the lives and lifestyles of a new breed of millionaires and billionaires, many of them self-made and from blue-collar backgrounds. He makes observations about their feelings and desires, and how their wealth has influenced them.)

Frankl, Viktor E., *Man's Search for Meaning*, Simon & Schuster Inc., 1984.
(Frankl survived a Nazi concentration camp. Here he describes the power of thoughts and attitudes.)

Furedi, Frank, *Paranoid Parenting*, Penguin Press, 2001.
(Furedi talks about the power of the media and its influences on parenting today.)

Gardner, Howard, Csikszentmihalyi, Mihaly, and Damon, William, *Good Work*, Basic Books, 2001.
(I took my quote in Chapter 6 about flow from this book, p. 5.)

Gendlin, Eugene T., *Focusing*, Bantam Books, 1978.

(Gendlin offers practical ways to help you focus on the present moment.)

Gerhardt, Sue, *Why Love Matters*, Brunner-Routledge, 2004.
(This is a well written and clear account of how early experience affects our reaction to stress throughout our lives.)

Gibran, Kahlil, *The Prophet*, Alfred Knopf, Inc., 1923.
(I've used quotes from this book in Chapter 6, pp. 53, 15 and 49, and Chapter 7, p. 49. This book has influenced my thinking more than any other.)

Gilbert, Daniel, *Stumbling on Happiness*, Harper Perennial, 2006.
(Gilbert tells readers how the human brain tries to predict how to be happy – and the many mistakes it makes. It's very enjoyable reading.)

Goleman, Daniel, *Emotional Intelligence: Why It Can Matter More Than IQ*, Bantam Books, 1995.
(The author discusses the importance of social connectedness and awareness.)

Hanh, Thich Nhat, *Old Path White Clouds: Walking in the Footsteps of Buddha*, Full Circle Publishing, 2003.
(This is a lovely account of the life of Buddha, and contains examples of mindfulness and meditation.)

Jacobson, Edmund, *Progressive Relaxation*, University of Chicago Press, 1938.
(This book provides a practical and clear description of deep relaxation. My graded relaxation method is based on the contents of *Progressive Relaxation*.)

James, Oliver, *Affluenza*, Vermilion, 2007.
(James tells us how modern culture and our 'needs' result in loss of contentment.)

Jeffers, Susan, *Feel the Fear and Do It Anyway*, Arrow Books, 1991.
(The author offers practical ways to overcome fears. It's very positive in tone.)

Jung, Carl, *Memories, Dreams and Reflections*, Fontana Paperbacks, 1983.

(This is Jung's beautifully written 'diary', in which he attempts to understand his own life.)

Kahneman, Daniel, Krueger, Alan B., Schkade, David, Schwartz, Norbert, and Stone, Arthur A. 'Would You Be Happier If You Were Richer? A Focusing Illusion', *Science*, 30 June 2006, pp. 1908–10.

(Kahneman and his colleagues asked people earning widely differing amounts of money to keep a questionnaire/diary about how they were feeling. The conclusion is that income doesn't much matter with regard to the flow of everyday experience.)

Knowles, Elizabeth, (ed.), *The Oxford Dictionary of Quotations*, sixth ed., Oxford University Press, 2004.

(I took quotes from this book for Chapter 3, p. 653, and the end of the book, p. 221.)

Padesky, Christine A., and Greenberger, Dennis, *Clinician's Guide to Mind over Mood*, The Guildford Press, 1995.

(The authors describe a number of practical ways to challenge and discard negative beliefs.)

Peale, Norman Vincent, *The Power of Positive Thinking*, Mandarin Paperbacks, 1959.

(This is one of the early books describing the power of attitudes and beliefs.)

Peck, M. Scott, *The Road Less Travelled*, Simon & Schuster, 1978.

(Peck defines love and talks about the importance of relationships. It's beautifully written, with interesting case studies.)

Persons, Jacqueline B., *Cognitive Therapy in Practice: A Case Formulation Approach*, W.W. Norton and Co., 1989.

(The author describes practical ways to challenge and discard negative beliefs.)

Ricard, Matthieu, *Happiness*, Atlantic Books, 2007.

(Ricard gives his definition of happiness. It might be helpful to compare it with my concept of contentment. He also suggests ways to learn to meditate.)

Rogers, Carl R., *On Becoming a Person*, Constable and Co. Ltd, 1961.

(Rogers defines his therapy/counselling approach. It emphasises collaboration between therapist and client, and is one of the first approaches that considers therapy to be more of a collaboration than a doctor–patient relationship.)

Rutter, Michael, 'Resilience in the Face of Adversity: Protective Factors and Resistance to Psychiatric Disorder', *British Journal of Psychiatry*, vol. 147, 1985, pp. 598–611.

(Rutter looks carefully at the factors that are associated with an ability to overcome adversity. It's quite an academic paper.)

Segal, Z.V., Williams, J.M.G., and Teasdale, J.D., *Mindfulness-Based Cognitive Therapy of Depression*, The Guildford Press, 2002.

(The authors describe practical ways to prevent relapse if you've been depressed. It's the only book I know that devotes itself entirely to dealing with relapse.)

Seligman, Martin, 'Depression and Learned Helplessness', in Friedman, R.J., and Katz, M.M. (eds), *The Psychology of Depression; Contemporary Theory and Research*, Winston-Wiley, 1974, pp. 83–113.

(Seligman describes in detail the relationship between thought and mood.)

Seligman, Martin, *Optimism: How to Change Your Mind and Your Life*, Simon & Schuster, 1900 and 1998.

(The author describes how optimistic and pessimistic mindsets come about, how you can learn to think optimistically and when it's best to do so.)

Servan-Schreiber, David, *Anticancer: A New Way of Life*, Michael Joseph, 2008.

(Although the book focuses primarily on how to deal wisely and optimistically with a diagnosis of cancer, it's truly remarkable in outlook. The sections on mindfulness, diet and exercise apply to all of us. It's beautifully written – a pleasure to read.)

Servan-Schreiber, David, *Healing Without Freud or Prozac*, Rodale International Ltd, 2004.

(The author offers practical, helpful ways to overcome low mood. It's very accessible and well written.)

Storr, Anthony, *Solitude*, HarperCollins, 1989.

(Storr considers our diversity with regard to the need for intimacy, using case studies of well-known individuals. It's very entertaining as well as informative.)

Tolle, Eckhart, *The Power of Now*, Hodder & Stoughton, 1999.

(This book sets out the relationship between focusing on the now and contentment. It also describes how to achieve mindfulness.)

Films

French Kiss, directed by Lawrence Kasdan for Twentieth Century Fox, 1995.

(This film contains a brilliant illustration of how thought blocking/distraction can help overcome fears and phobias – in this case, Meg Ryan's fear of flying.)

Hook, directed by Steven Spielberg for Universal (Amblin Entertainment), 1991.

(Peter has forgotten how to be in the present moment. This enjoyable film shows how he rediscovers this key to contentment.)

Now this is not the end.
It is not even the beginning of the end.
But it is, perhaps, the end of the beginning.

Speech at the Mansion House, 10 November 1942

Winston Churchill

Index